Barbecues & Grilling

Photography by David Matheson

Barbecues & Grilling

Antony Worrall Thompson
& Jane Suthering

KYLE CATHIE LTD

To my two Aussie boys, Blake and Sam, both experts in the art of the barbie.

Introduction

Barbies are very much a man thing; something to do with our time spent in caves, sitting around the camp fire, ripping chunks of flesh from recently roasted carcasses – the hunter gatherer, enjoying the spoils of the day. Then, as now, women didn't really get a look in.

Now we are seeing the renaissance of this ancient art that creates magical effects with the power of fire. Barbecuing is more popular, on a social rather than primitive level, but also as an everyday meal. I have to be honest though; the fare on offer is usually pretty uninspiring with most dishes involving sausages, chops, burgers and steaks. Supermarkets and butchers are trying a lot harder with marinades but for the most part, these have been commercially made, contain many unnatural products and are either too sweet or too sharp. And that's probably the reason you are buying this book – because you want to bring a little flair and imagination to your burgers and steaks, as well as experiment with more adventurous recipes.

Barbecuing is a great way to cook as long as you follow the rules. And there is more to it than just sticking meat on coals – if you have a kettle barbecue, try cooking with the lid down so that the food is permeated with a gorgeous smoky flavour. I will show you how to master these techniques as well as explaining the basics, from the equipment to the marinades and relishes, the preparation of the food and not forgetting the safety aspect.

Come rain or shine, barbecuing is not just a summer pursuit, so don't think you have to pack away your barbie at the beginning of autumn. I love cooking a roast with the lid down at any time of year, turning my back garden into an outdoor living room.

You can start with portable barbecues which can be taken on picnics and then responsibly disposed of and build up to mega barbies which are, in essence, a fully loaded outdoor kitchen. Al fresco cooking and dining puts people in the right mood, food appears to taste better and cooking is more like playing. Get out there and have fun, and guys, it's not just your domain, everyone can join in the fun.

Types of barbecue

There is so much choice for the barbie lover today. From disposable foil trays available in supermarkets and petrol stations to small, sturdy barbies for two as well as barbies in girlie colours to kick the boys into touch and stylish gas range barbies that are actually a second kitchen with extra cooking rings, there is something for everyone's style and pocket.

Before you go shopping, you must ask yourself what you want from your barbecue. Do you want a portable one that you can pack into a car and take on picnics? Or a permanent installation for your garden? Do you want to cook for large parties or family dinners? Are you keen to try different cooking techniques or want just a basic grate for grilling?

The most significant decision is whether you want a gas version (which is easy to operate, offers precision cooking and is brilliant for cooking for a large number of people) or whether you're going down the traditional route with charcoal, which requires a little more preparation and needs extra cleaning, but has the benefits of added flavour and all the romance of cooking with fire.

I've always been a fan of kettle grills, which are multi-purpose barbies with a domed lid that creates indirect heat with the lid down and direct heat over the charcoal or gas for simple grilling. These usually come with air vent controllers, a grate (preferably stainless steel or nickel plated) for the charcoal, a non-adjustable cooking rack and a vented cover. The vents in the lower bowl also act as sweepers which sweep the ash into the ash and grease catcher supported between the legs. This is probably one of the most popular barbies as it's easily transported with wheels on two of its three legs.

Gas barbies are stylish, sleek and modern. They come in large rectangular models, with up to 4 burning bars and separate rings for heating vegetables or sauces. These are excellent because they usually have adjustable racking heights so if you need to cook the food more slowly, the racks can be positioned further from the flames. They also have a raised narrow rectangular rack which keeps food, for example steaks, warm.

If you really want to get into barbecuing, it is worth considering building a permanent one of brick or stone. All you need is a tray for the charcoal and a grill rack, but you can customise it to suit your cooking needs and blend it in with your garden design.

So before purchasing your bbq, consider what you need. One of the key elements of a barbecue is the ability to control the height of the food over the charcoal or gas as this will ensure that you can cook food evenly. Check out the thickness of the steel, try out the vents, hinges, levers and all moving parts, look for handles that are easy to grasp and will remain cool during use. If you want a charcoal barbie, see if there is a cleaning system to help sweep up and clear away the ashes.

If you go for charcoal, you may well prefer the ubiquitous Hibachi (which means 'firebox' in Japanese) where the coals are laid on a grate rather than on the bottom of the barbie, brazier style. Hibachi barbecues are made from cast iron and are effective and exceptional value, but they're fairly primitive.

Fuel

Your choice – gas or charcoal. The purist would undoubtedly go for charcoal, but for convenience, as with many things in our world, gas is becoming the most popular choice. It's heat at your fingertips with the push of a button and no worries about how hot the barbecue is.

I don't want to appear flash, but I have both kinds; charcoal for the moments when I've thought about barbecuing well in advance and gas for that impulse barbie, when a few friends turn up unexpectedly. Whichever you prefer, you will need to have a good store of fuel.

When buying charcoal, always try to buy from local sources and look for charcoal that comes from coppiced woodlands – sustainable fuel from a renewable source.

Quality varies considerably – you can buy tiny pieces to large, good-sized chunks that last for a decent cooking period. Small chunks of charcoal are quite hard to light, smoke a lot to begin with and then burn down in no time. It is also worth spending money on better-quality charcoal as it will be smoke free, heats to a remarkable temperature and lasts for long enough to cook a good roast as well as simple grilling.

You may want to consider Greenheat briquettes which are stocked by many supermarkets and are made from olive stone. They achieve a decent temperature and are slow to burn (www.greenheat.com).

Most important of all, keep your charcoal dry – no matter how good it is, you won't be able to light it if it is damp!

If you have a gas barbecue, you will need propane gas cylinders. Make sure that you store and transport them upright, away from direct heat. Follow all the manufacturer's safety precautions and don't fill them more than 80 per cent full.

Essential equipment

Charcoal or gas cylinders

Wood chips to fragance the coals (see page 15)

Newspaper to act as a firelighter

Long matches

Poker

How to cook on a barbecue

People often ask me what they are doing wrong on the barbie – why does their food burn or dry out – and the answer usually lies in the heat of the barbecue, especially when charcoal is being used.

With gas, you just need to turn on the gas, press the button and you have instant heat that is easily controlled. Then you just need to keep an eye on what's going on with the food, but it's a lot trickier with charcoal, so this section will help you to manage the coals.

First things first. You must light the barbecue well in advance, a good half an hour before you want to start cooking. Lining the bottom of the charcoal tray with foil helps to reflect the heat upwards.

Try not to use firelighters as the smell will permeate your food. Instead use the old-fashioned method of newspaper, dry kindling and tapers. Never use petrol.

Once lit, LEAVE THE CHARCOAL ALONE until the flames have burned out and you are left with grey matter in bright sunlight and a deep glowing red in the evening.

Be prepared by organising your food well in advance (this applies to gas barbies as well), ideally the day before. You need time for marinating meat and fish as well as making relishes, salads, side dishes and desserts.

Lay out the food on manageable-sized trays or platters. If you are going to prepare food, especially meat and fish, in advance, keep it refrigerated, but remove 30 minutes before you want to begin cooking; you need the food to lose its fridge chill to help with the cooking time.

Wipe off any marinade before placing over the fire as the drips will create flare-ups which will burn the food; I always have a water spray on hand to douse the flames should they pop up – beer works too!

If you are cooking over indirect heat with the lid down, push the lit charcoal to the sides to allow a void in the centre over which you place the meat or fish to be roasted or cooked. Place a drip tray under the food to catch precious juices which can form the base of a good gravy or sauce. You will need to monitor the temperature carefully with a thermostat which is often in-built with the lid and you can regulate the temperature by using the vents – closing them to slow the cooking or opening them to increase the temperature.

Temperature guide

How can you tell what is the right temperature on which to cook your food? A difficult one to answer as fire has a mind of its own and barbecuing is an imprecise art of cookery. You will have many things to take into consideration including the quality of charcoal and how hot it will burn, the weather conditions (wind or rain will cool the lid and reduce the internal temperature of your cooking area). The more you use your barbecue, the more you will come to understand its ways.

This imprecision is why buying a decent barbie comes into focus; in order to maximise your control, you need to be able to regulate the height of the grill tray in relation to the heat source. If you can't, create an area of the barbecue that is a cool zone, where you have no heat or charcoal. This can either be achieved by having a heat-free zone around the whole perimeter and keeping the coals in the centre or treating the charcoal like a cake and leaving a wedge or slice without coals so that you have an area that is just warm.

A cool zone is vital for keeping food warm and resting it after cooking, especially for meat, much like you would after roasting. You should be able to hold your hand comfortably over this area almost indefinitely.

It is also important to have an area where you can thin the coals out to create a warm areas where food can finish off cooking. This is where raising the height of the grill tray or having a raised shelf will be invaluable. In simplistic terms you should be able to hold your hand over this area of the heat source for 8—10 seconds.

Then the hottest part of the barbecue can be created by mounding your charcoal to form a pyramid shape with the hottest part in the centre. This area of heat should be used for searing the meat or fish to crisp the surface before moving to another area to finish cooking. This hot area is perfect for cooking fish and rare meat as especially fish needs high heat to prevent it from sticking.

And remember most foods will benefit from cooking with the lid down which can shorten the cooking time by 25 per cent and also fragrance the food with a lovely smokey quality.

Setting up

As with the food, it is worth giving the barbecue area some forethought. If your garden is big enough, you might well have built a permanent barbecue area tastefully designed with built-in storage areas for logs, charcoal and kindling as well as an outdoor dining space.

But whether you have a custom-made area or wheel out your barbie when needed, you should give its location serious consideration. Make sure that the barbecue is situated away from overhanging branches or shrubs. If you have a portable barbecue, keep an eye on what the wind is doing – you don't want smoke blowing into either your house or your neighbours'.

The site needs to be flat and stable and ideally sheltered from the wind.

Make sure you have a clear path to the kitchen – the last thing you want is to stumble over an obstacle course between the fridge and barbecue.

A large counter top area made with limestone slabs or granite is excellent for laying out your food and accessories, but a brick wall or trestle table would perform that job nicely.

What would be ideal is a unit with drawers for keeping matches and tea towels, oven mitts and paper towels and even an area under the counter for a fridge, which may not even be used for food but is particularly useful for cold beers, wine and soft drinks.

You also need an area for rubbish – clearing plates, as well as ashes from charcoal barbecues, although these are great scattered over grass and flower beds when cold.

If choosing flooring, make sure it is easy to clean; wood decking is ok, but it does tend to become stained with grease spillages. I prefer a sealed stone floor which will weather well and is easy to brush and mop up.

Think carefully about lighting as there's nothing worse than cooking at night and not being able to see what you are cooking and worse – running the risk of serving up raw food!

There are plenty of portable garden lights available if you don't want to build in proper electrics (although I do think it is useful to have a couple of waterproof outdoor sockets for blenders and cocktail makers). Or hang fairy lights in trees or draped around your back wall, while garden candles are festive and scented ones can help keep the insects away.

Make sure that there is seating for your guests as well as places for them to put down plates and drinks – side tables, but upturned flower pots and tiles will also create flat surfaces.

Finally, fill buckets with ice and water to keep wine and soft drinks cool and choose some music to drift through the garden.

Preparation

A good barbie is down to the preparation; giving yourself enough time to prepare your food the day before, time to pack everything in neat tubs, covered from the elements, time to wash up all the bowls in which you've prepared salads and relishes.

The beauty of a real barbecue is that it represents what you enjoy eating and cooking. Don't buy ready marinated foods – they are pretty average and you can do better yourself without too much time or hassle.

Once your barbie is hot (about 30–45 minutes after lighting, depending on the quality of the charcoal and the amount you are using), brush the bars with a wire brush as most of the dirt or remnants of the last barbecue experience will have turned to dust. Another trick I use is to take a piece of beef suet or fat on the end of a skewer and rub it on the bars. Or lightly, but carefully, oil the grill with an oil spray – this will prevent food from sticking to the bars.

Then throw a handful of fragrant wood chips over the coals – I like apple, but you could also use hickory – or dried herbs such as rosemary, oregano or thyme to infuse your food with lovely aromas.

Overnight marinating will make an outstanding difference to your dishes, but always remember to remove the foods from the fridge before you wish to cook (about half an hour for fish and small pieces of meat and 1 hour for whole chickens and joints of meat). Marinating not only provides a wonderful flavour to the food but it also helps to tenderise as well.

Try a variety of foods – not just red meat, but firm fish, such as tuna, monkfish or salmon, and make sure that you have some veggie skewers and dishes – peppers, aubergine, onions, flat mushrooms and butternut squash all chargrill well.

Get your 'mis en place' ready – lay out your equipment (see page 18) and condiments on your table, so that everything is to hand when you are in the thick of the barbie.

Once the food is cooking, don't attempt to turn it until it is cooked and slightly charred – uncooked food will stick.

And if you're worried about the food being undercooked, buy a temperature probe or food thermostat. They are readily and cheaply available in cookshops... better safe than sorry.

And it's not just the food that counts, think about how you present the food. Whenever I'm abroad I'm always on the look out for exciting dishes, different-shaped plates and bowls, chunky unusual wooden salad bowls and wooden platters for large chunks of meat.

Barbecuing is a fun way to cook, so once you've got everything set up and your guests start to arrive, chill out and relax.

Safety first

Barbecues should be relaxed affairs. The food is fast and furious and the cooking method reminiscent of less sophisticated times. Enjoy this al fresco freedom, but never forget that you have to treat fire with respect.

Don't try to move your barbie once lit. Always have someone keeping an eye on it, and keep young children well away. Avoid loose clothing and make sure that any games or sport are played at a safe distance.

Keep a fire extinguisher or fire blanket to hand. If your gas barbecue catches fire, don't use a water-based extinguisher and always turn the gas off first.

Most food safety is common sense but common sense is often forgotten in the heat of the flames, so here are a few basic rules that will help you keep your family and friends safe from food poisoning.

Wash your hands thoroughly with hot, soapy water prior to the start of food preparation and after handling raw foods.

Use a separate chopping board for raw foods and scrub well after use with an anti-bacterial cleaning agent. I prefer wooden boards which have a natural antiseptic quality and are much easier to clean as bacteria doesn't tend to become lodged in the cuts.

Keep raw and cooked foods apart and never use the same plate to serve cooked food on as you used to store the raw food.

Keep hot foods hot and cold foods cold.

Defrost any frozen foods in the fridge, not at room temperature or under running hot water.

Always wash your knives thoroughly after using them for raw products and before using them on cooked foods.

Keep raw meats or poultry at the bottom of the fridge in covered containers.

Buy a meat probe or thermometer to test whether the meat, especially poultry, is cooked properly. Poultry needs to register at least 75°C/165°F to kill any salmonella or campylobacter bacteria.

Equipment

The first, most obvious and most important bit of kit you'll require is a good barbecue (see page 8). The choice is yours and much depends on your budget.

You will also need fuel (see page 9) and a prep table next to your barbecue as well as lighting, if you are barbecuing in the evening (see page 12).

Lastly there are many other useful pieces of equipment that you will need or that will make the barbecue safer and easier to handle, and it is worth making a checklist the day before as you don't want to find yourself short of a pair of tongs on the day.

Essential equipment

Wire brush – heavy duty to clean bars of the grills.

Tongs – buy American-style ones with scalloped edges and a long handle to prevent you burning your hands and arms.

Fire extinguisher or fire blanket.

Poker – to move coals around and create cool and warm areas (see page 11).

Shovel – to clean up the ashes.

Oven gloves or mitts – to protect your hands.

Plenty of oven cloths – for wiping down the bars of the grill.

Trays – for keeping food warm once the food is cooked.

A heavy-duty brush for basting the food during cooking.

A water spray – for dousing any flare-ups from dripping fat and marinades.

Hinged racks – square ones for turning toasted sandwiches and smaller foods such as sardines and scallops as well as skewers and burgers, or a fish-shaped one for cooking fish (which has a nasty tendency to stick to the grill).

Chopping boards – one for raw meat and one for cooked food.

Roasting fork or carving fork – very useful to save your fingers when slicing food.

Metal skewers – wooden ones are pleasant to look at but impractical because even when soaked in water they still seem to burn.

Kitchen scissors – always useful.

After the BBQ

A barbecue will last you several years if it's properly maintained. This is often easier said than done, as the last thing you want to do after a successful barbecue party is to clean all the equipment. But beware, if you don't, all the ashes will be solidified by rain, the grease from cooking becomes rancid, the griddle plates become rusty and your next barbecue won't be so successful.

Remember also to clear up the area, blow out the candles and collect bottles for recycling. If there is any left-over food, refrigerate it, but never keep uncooked meat that has been lying around for hours.

Always clean the barbecue after every use. Remove the ashes, brush the griddle bars, clean the grease from inside the hood and oil any moist surfaces to prevent rust.

If you are going to store your barbecue outside, I suggest you buy a cover for it to prevent weather damage. And I've said this before, but always make sure your charcoal store is dry.

With gas barbecues, always check the hose for blockages, nicks and cracking and disconnect it from the gas cylinder after use. Inspect the burners for irregular flame patterns and clean the gas jets if necessary.

If you are a fair-weather cook, give the barbie a good service before putting it away for the winter and when removing it from its winter slumbers be prepared to evacuate spiders, the occasional hibernating hedgehog and other outdoor treats.

Treat your barbecue with respect and it will give you many years of good service.

on the side

How to make crostini and bruschetta

Crostini are simple to make, and are great to serve with drinks or as a starter. Take a large French baguette bread and cut it, on the diagonal, into 5mm slices. Place on a tray and drizzle with extra virgin olive oil. Chargrill on the barbecue until crispy on both sides, then leave to cool. Cut a garlic clove in two and rub the crostini with the cut side.

Top the crostini with simple ingredients such as sliced cheese, salami or other cured meats, or pesto, or try tapenade (page 36) or aromatic aubergine purée (page 35).

Bruschetta is basically a thicker version of crostini, but because it's thicker, the centre of the bread will not become crisp. Cut a ciabatta bread in half lengthways, and if wished, into suitable-sized serving pieces. Prepare as for crostini.

How to heat pitta and other flat breads

Lightly toast the bread directly on the barbecue grill. Alternatively, wrap the bread in foil and place on the coolest part of the grill for a few minutes. If you have a barbecue with a lid, close the lid.

american spicy chicken wings

You can buy skinned chicken wings from some butchers, which are great for this recipe as they go crispy on the barbecue. Removing the skin also reduces the amount of flaring of the flames during cooking.

Serves 6

Set the chicken wing pieces in a hinged wire rack and cook them over medium-hot coals on the barbecue grill for 15–20 minutes or until golden, crispy and thoroughly cooked.

In a large bowl, mix together the melted butter, ketchup and Tabasco. Toss the wings in this mixture, then dust with cayenne pepper and salt, to taste. Serve hot, with blue cheese dip (see page 134).

12 chicken wings (about 1kg), cut in half, wing tips discarded

50g unsalted butter, melted

2 tablespoons tomato ketchup

1 teaspoon tabasco

cayenne pepper

salt and freshly ground black pepper

sweet and spicy chicken wings

It is worth marinating the chicken wings for as long as possible to allow the flavours to penetrate. Set them in a hinged metal rack for easy turning during cooking.

Serves 6–8

In a food processor, blend the Szechwan pepper, garlic, ginger, orange zest, spring onions and chilli to a rough paste. Add the honey, soy and oils and whizz to a fairly smooth consistency. Season generously with salt and freshly ground black pepper and transfer to a large bowl. Add the chicken pieces and mix well until evenly coated. Cover and leave to marinate in the fridge for at least 4 hours, preferably up to 24 hours, turning occasionally. Remove from the fridge at least 30 minutes before cooking to bring the chicken to room temperature.

Drain the chicken pieces from the marinade and cook on the barbecue grill for 7–8 minutes on each side until thoroughly cooked and lightly charred. They should be tender when tested with a skewer.

20 chicken wings (about 1.6kg), cut in half through the joint, tips discarded

For the marinade:

2 tablespoons Szechwan peppercorns, toasted in a dry frying pan then ground

1 tablespoon chopped garlic

3 tablespoon finely chopped fresh ginger

3 tablespoons grated orange zest (about 4 large oranges)

4 spring onions, chopped

1 chilli, deseeded and chopped

2 tablespoons clear honey

2 tablespoons soy sauce

150ml vegetable oil

50ml toasted sesame oil

gorgonzola figs with pancetta

8 large ripe figs

125g gorgonzola cheese, cut into 8 pieces

a few sprigs of thyme

16 slices pancetta or thin-cut streaky bacon

freshly ground black pepper

Vary the cheese to suit your taste – tallegio melts well, feta is another good partner. For a substantial starter, serve two pancetta-wrapped figs per person with a rocket salad.

Make a criss-cross incision in the top of each fig and gently squeeze open slightly. Insert a piece of gorgonzola and some thyme leaves, and grind over some black pepper.

Wrap each fig with two slices of pancetta or streaky bacon. Secure with a cocktail stick or fine skewer.

Set the figs on a hot barbecue, or on a griddle pan on the barbecue, and allow to cook for 3–5 minutes until the pancetta is crispy and the figs are warm and tender inside.

tuna and bean salad

2 x 400g tins of cannellini beans, drained

2 x 185g tins tuna in oil, flaked

1 medium red onion, thinly sliced

2 tablespoons roughly chopped flat-leaf parsley

4 tablespoons extra virgin olive oil

1–2 tablespoons lemon juice or wine vinegar

salt and freshly ground black pepper

This is a really healthy salad and so easy to make. It's also a recipe for a short-notice barbecue as you will probably have most of the ingredients in your cupboard. Serve with garlic bread.

In a large bowl, combine all the ingredients except the oil and vinegar. Mix the oil and 1 tablespoon of vinegar together, toss through the salad and season to taste, adding extra lemon juice or vinegar, if wished.

hot chilli chicken fajitas

4 skinless and boneless chicken breasts

1 tablespoon paprika

½ tablespoon chilli powder

1 teaspoon golden caster sugar

finely grated zest and juice of 1 lime

2 tablespoons chilli oil

To serve:

tomato and avocado salsa (see page 139)

8 medium wheat flour tortillas, warmed

shredded iceberg lettuce

142ml carton soured cream

This Mexican favourite is great for outdoor eating and you can experiment with different meat and poultry as well as vegetarian options using peppers, mushrooms and tofu.

Cut each chicken breast lengthways into 8 strips and transfer to a large bowl. Stir in the paprika, chilli powder, sugar, lime zest and juice and the chilli oil. Cover and leave to marinate for at least 1–2 hours, or up to 24 hours in the fridge. Remove from the fridge at least 30 minutes before cooking.

Meanwhile, soak 16 bamboo skewers. Thread 2 pieces of chicken onto each skewer. Place on the barbecue over hot coals and cook for 2–3 minutes on each side until cooked through.

Place the chicken skewers on a serving plate and hand around the tomato and avocado salsa, warmed tortillas, lettuce and soured cream, and allow each person to assemble their fajita.

Makes 8

barbecue pork with barbecue dressing

3 pork fillets or tenderloins

7 tablespoons barbecue
spice blend (see below)

barbecue dressing (see
below)

For the barbecue spice blend:

2 teaspoons cumin seeds

1 teaspoon chilli powder

2 teaspoons curry powder

2 teaspoons salt

2 tablespoons paprika

1 tablespoon freshly ground
white pepper

2 tablespoons unrefined
soft brown sugar

For the barbecue dressing:

1 tablespoon extra virgin
olive oil

2 tablespoons barbecue
spice blend

6 tablespoons mayonnaise

6 tablespoons soured
cream

6 tablespoons buttermilk

This barbecue pork recipe can be served with the cabbage and jicama salad (page 121) to make a fab side dish or starter, or you could simply mix it with salad leaves of your choice.

To prepare the spice blend, dry-fry the cumin seeds in a frying pan then grind them with a mortar and pestle or spice mill. Dry-fry the chilli and curry powders in a frying pan, stirring all the time so that they toast but do not burn. Combine all the ingredients, except the sugar. Set 2 tablespoons aside for the dressing, then stir the sugar into the remaining mixture.

To prepare the barbecue dressing, combine the olive oil and reserved 2 tablespoons of unsweetened spice blend in a small pan and heat it until it becomes aromatic. Leave it to cool slightly then stir into the mayonnaise, with the soured cream and buttermilk. Cover and chill until required.

When you are ready to cook the meat, remove any fat and sinew from the pork tenderloins and rub each with 2 tablespoons of the sweetened spice blend. Grill the pork on the barbecue grill, turning occasionally, for 20–25 minutes until cooked through.

Let the meat rest for 5–10 minutes, then cut each tenderloin, at an angle, into thick slices.

Alternatively, wrap in a double thickness of kitchen foil and cook on the barbecue, turning frequently for a similar time. Remove from the foil and sear directly on the grill for 2–3 minutes.

Serve slices of the pork with the barbecue dressing as a dip, or with cabbage and jicama salad, or a salad of your choice, and drizzle the barbecue dressing over the pork.

Scallops are my first choice for this recipe, but chunks of monkfish, large green-lipped mussels or smoked oysters are also good. If you are using bacon, stretch each rasher with the back of a knife to make it thinner.

Remove the small, tough piece of gristle on the side of each scallop, then rinse them and pat dry on kitchen paper or a clean tea towel.

Put the scallops in a small bowl with the oil and thyme leaves and season generously with pepper. Turn them until evenly coated.

Wrap a rasher of pancetta or bacon around each scallop and secure with a cocktail stick. Cover and refrigerate for up to 8 hours. Remove from the fridge at least 30 minutes before cooking.

Set the scallops on the barbecue over hot coals and cook for 1–2 minutes each side until the pancetta or bacon is crispy. Serve at once.

Makes 16

wrapped scallops

16 large scallops, roes removed if preferred

1 tablespoon vegetable oil

2 teaspoons thyme leaves

freshly ground black pepper

16 rashers pancetta or streaky bacon

salad leaves to serve (optional)

Here's one for the more adventurous barbecue cook. Squid is perfect for the barbecue as it can cope with the fierce heat and smoky flavour and takes no more than a minute or so to cook.

Cut the squid flesh into 3cm pieces. Cut any tentacles in half through the base. Set a lightly oiled frying pan or metal tray on the barbecue over high heat and when it's hot, add the squid and cook just until opaque, about 1 minute. Alternatively, cook on the stove over high heat. Allow to cool to room temperature.

In a large bowl, whisk together the oil, vinegar, garlic, oregano, ½ teaspoon salt and the crushed chillies. Stir in the squid, celery, olives and parsley. Cover and chill for 1 hour or overnight. Just before serving, stir the salad and season to taste.

Serves 6–8

squid, olive and celery salad

900g prepared squid

100ml extra virgin olive oil

3 tablespoons red wine vinegar

1 garlic clove, finely chopped

½ teaspoon dried oregano

¼ teaspoon crushed dried chillies

2 celery stalks, thinly sliced

75g stoned green olives, sliced

2 tablespoons chopped flat-leaf parsley

salt and freshly ground pepper

pissaladiere toast

extra virgin olive oil, for frying and drizzling

4 onions, thinly sliced

2 garlic cloves, finely diced

4 teaspoons thyme leaves

4 tomatoes, deseeded and sliced

2 tablespoons stoned black olives, sliced

dash of balsamic vinegar

8 small slices of country bread

8 anchovy fillets, halved lengthways (optional)

12 basil leaves, finely shredded, to garnish

freshly ground black pepper

This makes a sophisticated starter, perfect for a garden lunch. If you have vegetarian guests, you can leave out the anchovy, but it does add a saltiness to the onions.

Heat 4 tablespoons of olive oil in a pan or frying pan, and cook the onions, garlic and thyme over a medium-low heat until the onions are very soft and golden in colour – about 25 minutes. Add the tomatoes and olives and combine well. Season with a dash of balsamic vinegar and plenty of black pepper.

Drizzle the slices of bread with a little olive oil and chargrill them on both sides. While the bread is still on the barbecue, spoon on the onion mixture and arrange strips of anchovy on top, if using.

Garnish with basil and serve immediately.

chargrilled thai beef salad

Serves 4

Prepare the steak and other ingredients well in advance as you will need to barbecue the meat first and then marinate it for 2 hours. Then toss the salad just before serving. Serve with plenty of crunchy lettuce.

Set a dry frying pan over medium heat. Add the rice and toast until golden but not burned. Grind the rice in a clean coffee-grinder or pound to a powder with a pestle and mortar, and set aside.

Reheat the frying pan and add the dried red chillies. Toast until they are smoky, then grind or pound to a powder and set aside.

Chargrill the beef over a direct heat on the barbecue grill for about 5 minutes, turning regularly, until well marked outside and rare to medium-rare inside. Alternatively, cook on a ridged grill pan over high heat. Transfer to a plate. Combine the sesame oil with the sweet soy sauce and brush over the fillet. Cover and leave to marinate in the fridge for up to 2 hours.

Place the sugar in a small bowl, stir in the lime juice to dissolve and add the fish sauce. Mix in half a teaspoon of the reserved ground dried chilli powder and half a teaspoon of the ground rice and set aside.

Place the cucumber in a large bowl and mix in the shallots, cherry tomatoes, fresh red chillies, herbs and spring onions. Add the lime juice mixture and toss to combine.

Slice the beef thinly and toss it through the salad, along with any cooking juices that have collected on the plate. You can add extra ground rice to thicken the juices and more dried chilli to increase the spiciness, if liked.

1 tablespoon uncooked jasmine rice

2 dried red chillies, seeds removed, if wished

500g thick fillet steak

2 tablespoons toasted sesame oil

5 tablespoons sweet soy sauce (katchup manis)

2 teaspoons golden caster sugar

4 tablespoons lime juice

3 tablespoons fish sauce (nam pla)

1 small cucumber, peeled, halved lengthways, deseeded and cut into 1cm thick slices

4 red shallots, thinly sliced

12 cherry tomatoes, halved

2 fresh red chillies, deseeded and thinly sliced

a handful of mint leaves

a handful of coriander leaves

a small handful of ripped basil leaves

4 spring onions, thinly sliced

2 large aubergines

4 tablespoons extra virgin olive oil, for brushing

1 red onion, finely chopped

3 tablespoons chopped mint

1 teaspoon ground cumin

250g soft goat's cheese

salt and freshly ground black pepper

vegetable raita, to serve (see page 135)

aubergine and goat's cheese parcels

Yum! What could be more delicious – aubergine, goat's cheese and olive oil. This is a wonderful Mediterranean recipe, though the raita will give it a spicy zing.

Soak 16 wooden cocktail sticks in cold water for 30 minutes. Using a sharp knife, top and tail the aubergines and cut each one lengthways into eight slices, discarding the end pieces. Brush each slice with olive oil on both sides and season well.

Barbecue the aubergine slices for 5–6 minutes until golden and soft on each side. Meanwhile, combine the onion, mint and cumin in a small bowl and cut the goat's cheese into 16 pieces.

Spread a piece of cheese on a slice of aubergine and scatter with some of the onion mixture, then roll up and secure with a cocktail stick. Repeat the process with the remaining slices.

Place the aubergine rolls on the barbecue and grill for about 4 minutes, turning once. Serve warm, with the vegetable raita for dipping.

goat's cheese in vine leaves

If you can find fresh vine leaves, first blanch them in boiling water then refresh in iced water. Choose the smaller varieties of goat's cheese, such as Crottin de Chavignol.

Makes 6

Lay the vine leaves out flat and place a goat's cheese in the centre of each one. Sprinkle the cheese with oregano leaves and pepper and drizzle a little olive oil over each one. Fold the leaves over to enclose the cheese.

Set the parcels on a tray, seam-side down and refrigerate for up to 24 hours. Remove from the fridge 30 minutes before cooking.

Cook the parcels on the barbecue over medium coals for about 5 minutes on each side until the leaves are slightly crispy ands the cheese is warmed. Serve with chutney and a sprinkling of roasted walnuts, if liked.

6 large vine leaves, fresh (see intro) or from a packet

6 individual firm goat's cheeses such as Crottin de Chavignol

1 tablespoon oregano leaves

freshly ground black pepper

olive oil for drizzling

sweet chutney, such as fig, to serve (optional)

walnut pieces, roasted (optional)

aromatic aubergine purée

This spicy aubergine purée is wonderful with flat bread, or served as a dip with belgian endive leaves. Mirin is a Japanese spirit-based liquid sweetener, available in Asian stores and supermarkets.

Serves 4–6

Prick the aubergines all over with a fork and set them on a baking tray. Cook them on the barbecue grill over hot coals for 30–40 minutes, with the lid down if you have one, until completely collapsed, turning once or twice during cooking. Alternatively, cook in a pre-heated oven at 190°C/375°F/gas mark 5.

Split the cooked aubergines lengthways and scoop out the flesh, discarding the skin. Mash the flesh with a fork.

In a small frying pan heat the vegetable oil, then add the garlic, ginger, spring onions and chilli flakes and stir-fry for 30 seconds. Add the soy sauce, sugar, vinegar and mirin or sherry, and stir to combine. Cook for 1 minute.

Fold in the aubergine purée and cook over a low heat, stirring frequently, for about 15 minutes or until most of the moisture has evaporated.

Remove from the heat and when slightly cool, fold in the sesame oil and coriander leaves. If you want a milder flavour, when completely cold fold in the yogurt.

1kg aubergines

3 tablespoons vegetable oil

2 tablespoons finely chopped garlic

1 tablespoon grated ginger

8 spring onions, chopped

½ teaspoon crushed dried chillies

5 tablespoons light soy sauce

4 tablespoons unrefined soft dark brown sugar

1 tablespoon rice wine vinegar

2 tablespoons mirin or dry sherry

1 teaspoon sesame oil

1 tablespoon chopped coriander leaves

4 tablespoons Greek-style yogurt (optional)

garlic bread

1 head garlic

extra virgin olive oil, to drizzle

250g unsalted butter, softened

4 tablespoons chopped parsley (optional)

2 French baguette breads, cut in half, crossways

salt and freshly ground black pepper

Serves 8

For garlic bread, you need garlic butter. For a simple garlic butter, just crush 4 garlic cloves with a little salt and mix with 250g butter. Both versions of the butter can be kept in the fridge for up to a week, or the freezer for up to a month.

Preheat the oven to 190°C/375°F/gas mark 5. Cut the tops off the whole heads of garlic to expose the tops of the individual cloves. Set the head on double thickness pieces of kitchen foil, drizzle them with oil and season lightly. Wrap carefully and roast for 35–45 minutes until tender. Leave to cool.

Separate the cloves and squeeze out the pulp. Mix with the softened butter, adding the parsley if using. Season to taste. If not using the garlic butter immediately, set it on a sheet of clingfilm or kitchen foil and roll into a log, then refrigerate or freeze until required.

Without cutting all the way through the bread, slice at 3cm intervals, to four fifths of the way through, and insert some garlic butter in between the cuts. Wrap each baguette in foil and cook on the barbecue, turning occasionally, for about 15 minutes until heated through.

tapenade

100g capers, drained and rinsed

1 x 50g tin anchovy fillets, drained and diced

1 teaspoon Dijon mustard

12 basil leaves, ripped

6 tablespoons extra virgin olive oil

500g pitted black olives marinated in olive oil, drained and stoned

1 tablespoon red wine vinegar

3 tablespoons chopped parsley

freshly ground black pepper

Makes about 675g

Based on olives, capers and anchovies, this is great spread on crostini or bruschetta. It will keep, covered, in the fridge for up to to 1 month, so you can keep nibbling long after the barbecue ends.

Combine all the ingredients except the parsley and the pepper in a food-processor and whizz until roughly puréed, allowing some texture to remain. Then stir in the parsley and add pepper to taste.

Asparagus is traditionally steamed, but I love the woody taste of the chargrilled stems. Simple to prepare, but very elegant, this recipe should be served on a long platter for full effect.

Makes 16

Remove the tough ends of the asparagus spears by breaking about 3cm off the stem end. Peel the asparagus, if wished, and blanch in boiling salted water for 2 minutes. Drain and refresh in iced water, then drain and dry thoroughly. Place in a shallow dish.

In a bowl, combine the olive oil, basil, thyme, parsley and spring onion. Mix together and pour over the asparagus. Allow to marinate for at least 30 minutes, or overnight.

Wrap each asparagus spear in a slice of prosciutto.

Set the asparagus on the barbecue. Grill for 5–6 minutes, turning occasionally, until the ham is crispy. Season to taste with black pepper.

grilled asparagus in crispy prosciutto

16 large asparagus spears

3 tablespoons extra virgin olive oil

8 large basil leaves, chopped

1 teaspoon chopped thyme

1 tablespoon chopped parsley

1 spring onion, finely chopped

16 slices prosciutto (Parma ham)

salt and freshly ground black pepper

on the rack

How to barbecue steaks

Start by choosing the right steaks. It's fat and age that give the beef its flavour, so choose steaks that have small rivulets of fat running through them – this is known as marbling. Suitable cuts include sirloin, rump, T-bone, rib-eye and fillet, and they should be at least 3cm thick. It's better to cook a large steak for two people and cut it on the diagonal than have two small, dry steaks.

Brush the steak with vegetable oil and season with pepper only (sprinkle with salt just prior to cooking as it draws out the meat's natural moisture). Sear the steak on both sides on the hottest part of the barbecue grill for 1 minute to seal each side, then continue grilling as outlined below. It's always difficult to be precise about the timing, because it depends on the thickness of the steak and the heat of the barbecue, so after the initial sealing, as a guide allow:

for pink, 1 minute more each side
for well cooked, 2–3 minutes each side

Transfer the steaks to a plate. Leave to rest for 3–5 minutes to allow the juices to settle before eating.

Marinades; yes or no?

Marinades act as a flavour enhancer and tenderiser, and are usually made up of four parts red wine (or red wine vinegar or citrus juice) to one part oil – almost the reverse of a salad dressing. Flavouring ingredients such as herbs, seeds and chopped vegetables can also be added.

Marinades are most effective for slightly tough cuts of meat such as onglet, a popular French cut of beef steak best represented by the English cut 'skirt' taken from the inside of the ribs, or for larger cuts of meat.

If you are marinating steaks, cover them and leave for at least 2–3 hours, or overnight, in the fridge. Bring them out to room temperature at least 30 minutes before cooking, and shake off any excess marinade before setting on the barbecue grill.

How to barbecue sausages

Small sausages are easier to handle if arranged in a hinged grill rack. Large sausages can be cooked directly on the barbecue grill. Always ensure that they are set high enough so that flames caused by the dripping fat do not touch the sausages. Cook over medium-high heat, turning occasionally, until evenly browned on all sides – about 10–12 minutes.

How to barbecue chops

Trim excess fat from the chops and cut through the remaining fat at regular intervals – this stops the edges curling up. Marinate the meat if you like, or brush with oil and season with pepper (not salt) or your chosen spices.

Place pork chops on the hottest part of the barbecue grill and sear for 2 minutes on each side, then move to a medium-hot area and cook for a further 5–7 minutes each side.

Place lamb chops over high heat and sear for 1 minute each side, then move to a medium heat and cook for a further 3–5 minutes each side.

How to spatchcock

To open out small fowl such as quail and poussin, cut each side of the backbone with scissors or poultry shears and discard the bone. Open out the bird skin-side up and flatten with the heel of your hand.

How to calculate cooking time

On the barbecue, it's more about thickness than weight. Allow 15 minutes per 2–3cm thickness for joints of meat and increase by 5 minutes for a whole leg of lamb. For fish, allow 3 minutes per 2–3cm, about 15–20 minutes each side for a whole fish such as salmon and 10–15 minutes for a smaller whole fish such as bass or bream.

red chilli and ginger butter

Great for fish or shellfish. Keeps in the fridge for a week or the freezer for three months.

1 tablespoon finely chopped red chilli
1 tablespoon finely grated fresh ginger
½ tablespoon finely grated lime zest
1 tablespoon lime juice
250g unsalted butter, diced then
softened to room temperature
salt and ground white pepper

Combine all the ingredients in a bowl, seasoning with about 1 teaspoon each of salt and ground white pepper, and beat well until smooth. Transfer to a sheet of clingfilm or kitchen foil and roll into a log about 3cm in diameter. Chill or freeze until required.

Alternatively, warm all the ingredients together in a small saucepan and pour over your chosen barbecued food.

Makes about 275g

roquefort butter

The saltiness and tang of blue cheese makes this a great accompaniment for steaks and burgers. You could use stilton or any other blue cheese as an alternative to roquefort. Keeps for a week in the fridge, or three months in the freezer.

150g roquefort cheese, crumbled
150g unsalted butter, diced then
softened to room temperature

2 tablespoons snipped chives
freshly ground black pepper

Beat all the ingredients together until fairly smooth and use straight away. Alternatively transfer to a sheet of clingfilm or kitchen foil and roll into a log about 3cm in diameter, then refrigerate or freeze until required.

Makes about 300g

anchovy butter

This will keep in the fridge for a week or freezer for three months. Delicious with white fish or steak.

1 tablespoon snipped fresh chives
2 teaspoons Dijon mustard
2 tablespoons chopped basil
12 anchovy fillets in oil, roughly
chopped with 1 tablespoon of
their oil
25g capers
finely grated zest and juice of 1 lemon
1 sweet and sour pickled cucumber,
finely chopped
250g unsalted butter, diced and
softened to room temperature
freshly ground black pepper

In a food-processor, pulse together the chives, mustard, basil, anchovies, capers, lemon zest and juice, the pickled cucumber and ½ teaspoon pepper until roughly blended. With the machine running, add the butter piece by piece until thoroughly combined, scraping down the sides of the container from time to time.

Transfer the butter to a sheet of clingfilm or kitchen foil and roll into a log about 3cm in diameter. Refrigerate or freeze until ready to use.

Makes about 300g

tomato and green peppercorn butter

A great butter to serve with steaks – or simply spread on hot toast! It will keep for a week in the fridge or three months in the freezer.

2 garlic cloves, finely chopped
4 sun-dried tomatoes, drained and
finely chopped
1 tablespoon green peppercorns in
brine, drained
2 teaspoons very finely chopped
rosemary
2 tablespoons parsley leaves, blanched
for 1 minute in boiling salted water,
then well drained
1 tablespoon lemon juice
250g unsalted butter, diced and
softened to room temperature
salt

In a food-processor, pulse together the garlic, tomatoes, peppercorns, herbs, lemon juice and about ½ teaspoon salt until roughly blended. Add the butter and pulse just until combined.

Transfer the butter to a sheet of clingfilm or kitchen foil and roll into a log about 3cm in diameter. Refrigerate or freeze until ready to use.

Makes about 300g

salsa verde butter

If you enjoy salsa verde (an Italian herb sauce), have a roll of this butter ready, so that you can pop a slice onto your barbecued meat or fish. It keeps in the fridge for a week, in freezer for a month.

12 spinach leaves

1 small bunch watercress, leaves only

1 tablespoon tarragon leaves

4 tablespoons parsley leaves

4 tablespoons chervil leaves

4 shallots, chopped

4 cornichons, rinsed and chopped

6 anchovy fillets

3 tablespoons capers, rinsed then well drained

2 garlic cloves, roughly chopped

½ teaspoon cayenne pepper

5 hard-boiled egg yolks

2 large raw egg yolks

250g unsalted butter, at room temperature

125ml extra virgin olive oil

2 teaspoons white wine vinegar

salt and freshly ground black pepper

In a large pan of boiling water, blanch the spinach, watercress, herbs and shallots for 1 minute, then drain, refresh under cold water and squeeze dry.

Put the spinach mixture in a food-processor. Add the cornichons, anchovies, capers, garlic, cayenne pepper and salt and pepper. Process to a smooth paste.

Add the hard-boiled and raw egg yolks and the butter and process again until thoroughly mixed. Add the oil little by little, until the mixture is smooth and glossy. Beat in the vinegar and add more salt and pepper to taste.

Transfer the butter to a sheet of clingfilm or kitchen foil and roll into a log about 3cm in diameter. Refrigerate or freeze until ready to use.

Makes approximately 400g

sesame & mustard rub

This spicy paste will bring out the flavour of fish fillets, chicken portions and pork chops.

1 teaspoon cayenne pepper

2 teaspoons black mustard seeds

4 garlic cloves, chopped

finely grated zest and juice of 2 limes

2 tablespoons toasted sesame oil

salt

Put the cayenne in a mortar, add the mustard seeds and a generous pinch of salt, and grind with a pestle. Work in the garlic, lime zest and juice and sesame oil to make a fairly smooth paste.

Alternatively, whizz all the ingredients in a liquidiser goblet or small food-processor until fairly smooth.

Rub the paste over your chosen fish or meat at least 1 hour before cooking on the barbecue.

Serves 6

You need to start this recipe a day ahead of eating it. If you want to double the recipe then prepare two small joints of pork and not one large one – the cooking time will then be the same for both joints.

Cut the excess fat from the pork then butterfly it by cutting almost in half and opening out. Press down firmly with the heel of your hand to give an even thickness of meat.

Combine the dry-rub ingredients. Rub this mixture thoroughly all over the surface of the pork then place it in a plastic container, covered, in the fridge for at least 4, and up to 24 hours. Remove the pork from the fridge about 1 hour before cooking to allow it to come to room temperature.

Place the pork on the barbecue over medium-hot coals and cook for 30–40 minutes with the lid down if you have one, turning regularly.

Transfer the pork to a large sheet of double thickness kitchen foil and set it back on the barbecue. In a small bowl, combine the tequila, stock, treacle, chillies, garlic and chilli sauce and pour the mixture over the meat. Close the foil tightly. Continue to cook the pork for a further 30 minutes until thoroughly cooked when tested. Leave to cool then pour the liquid that has accumulated in the foil into a bowl.

When the meat is cool enough to handle, shred it and toss with the reserved liquid. Arrange the meat on a platter with the cheese, tomatoes, onion and avocados.

Serve with the warm tortillas and invite everyone to build their own burrito with the meat and accompaniments. Roll the tortillas and eat immediately.

Variation

For melt-in-the-mouth pork, prepare the joint with the rub as above then place it in a saucepan and cover with 300ml orange juice and 300ml water. Cover and simmer for 2 hours or cook in the oven at 160°C/325°F/gas mark 3. Leave to cool in the liquid. Prepare the tequila mix as above, but replacing the chicken stock with an equal quantity of the cooking liquid.

Drain the meat and pat dry on kitchen paper, then place in a metal tin on the barbecue. Pour the tequila mixture over, then baste and turn the meat occasionally until lightly charred on all sides. Continue as above.

1kg boneless pork shoulder

5 tablespoons tequilla

5 tablespoons chicken stock

1 tablespoon black treacle

2 dried chillies, finely chopped

2 garlic cloves, finely chopped

1 tablespoons hot chilli sauce

175g mild cheddar cheese, grated

3 plum tomatoes, chopped

1 medium red onion, chopped

2 ripe Haas avocados, peeled and sliced

4–6 wheatflour tortillas, warmed

For the dry-rub mixture:

2 tablespoons paprika

2 teaspoon dried oregano

2 teaspoons ground cumin

2 teaspoons garlic powder

1 tablespoon each salt and ground black pepper

pork fillet 'chimichurri'

2 pork fillets (tenderloin),
fat and sinew removed

2 garlic cloves, sliced

8 slices Parma ham,
or similar cured ham

For the marinade:

2 large garlic cloves, finely
chopped

½ tablespoon coarsely
chopped oregano

½ tablespoon chopped
flat-leaf parsley

2 anchovy fillets, mashed

1 red chilli, deseeded and
finely chopped

2 tablespoons sweet chilli
sauce

2 tablespoons sherry vinegar

3 tablespoons extra virgin
olive oil

100ml chicken stock

Chimichurri is a great Argentinian sauce based on garlic, parsley, olive oil and as much chilli as you like. It goes well with beef steaks as well as pork and chicken.

To make the marinade, whisk together all the ingredients in a saucepan and slowly bring to the boil. Remove from the heat and leave to go cold.

Make several incisions all over the meat and insert slices of garlic. Place in a dish and pour over the marinade, then cover and leave in the fridge for at least 3 hours or preferably overnight. Allow to come to room temperature for about 30 minutes before cooking.

Drain and pat dry each pork fillet, then wrap in ham and secure with wooden cocktail sticks. Oil the barbecue grill, then char-grill the pork on a medium-hot barbecue for 20–25 minutes, turning regularly and basting the pork with the marinade. Test to check that the meat is fully cooked (no longer pink inside) then leave to rest for 10 minutes.

Slice the pork fillets thickly and serve.

Serves 4–6

barbecued leg of lamb

It's quite easy to 'butterfly' a leg of lamb, and all you need is a sharp knife: simply cut the leg almost in half horizontally, removing the bone as you go. Then open out the lamb – as if opening a book – and press it flat. If this sounds too daunting, I'm sure your butcher will butterfly the lamb for you. Make sure you pat the lamb dry with kitchen paper before setting it on the barbecue. Once the fat hits the coals it will start to flame so put the lid down until the flames subside.

Place the lamb in a dish or other container large enough to hold it and the marinade. Combine all the ingredients for the marinade with 600ml cold water and pour over the meat. Cover and refrigerate overnight (even up to 48 hours), or leave for two to three hours at room temperature.

Bring the lamb to room temperature if refrigerated. Remove the lamb from the marinade and pat dry. Pour off and discard the watery part of the marinade and reserve the rest for basting.

Grill on a hot barbecue for 15–20 minutes on each side for pink lamb, 20–30 for well-done, basting the lamb with marinade during cooking.

Leave to rest for 10 minutes then cut in thick slices to serve.

Serves 6

1 large leg of lamb, boned and butterflied

For the marinade:

150ml olive oil

6 tablespoons roughly chopped oregano or mint

8 garlic cloves, finely chopped

1 tablespoon paprika

1 teaspoon crushed dried chilli flakes

2 teaspoons ground cumin

3 bay leaves, finely chopped

1 tablespoon salt

2 teaspoons freshly ground black pepper

chargrilled barnsley chops

Barnsley chops are also known as double lamb chops as they are cut from the whole saddle of the lamb. Hungarian relish (page 140) makes a perfect accompaniment.

Season the chops with salt and pepper and brush with olive oil. Cook on the barbecue grill over hot coals for about 8 minutes each side, until the fat is crispy. Sprinkle with thyme leaves and leave to rest for 5 minutes before serving.

Serves 6

6 Barnsley chops, about 350g each

extra virgin olive oil

fresh thyme leaves

salt and freshly ground black pepper

24 raw jumbo prawns

For the marinade:

5cm piece of fresh ginger, peeled and grated

a small bunch of coriander, chopped

12 mint leaves, chopped

2 green chillies, deseeded and finely diced

4 garlic cloves, crushed with a little salt to a smooth paste

4 tablespoons fish sauce (nam pla)

2 tablespoons sweet chilli sauce

4 tablespoons toasted sesame oil

2 tablespoons light soy sauce

2 tablespoons rice wine vinegar

1 teaspoon dried shrimp paste (blachan)

juice of 2 limes

4 fresh lime leaves, finely chopped

You can also flavour fish with this marinade – just replace the prawns with fillets or small steaks of firm fish such as mackerel, seabass, salmon or monkfish.

Combine all the marinade ingredients and marinate the prawns for 30–60 minutes in the fridge.

Remove the prawns from the fridge about 30 minutes before you want to cook them. Place them in a hinged metal rack if you have one and cook on the barbecue grill over high heat for 2–3 minutes each side, basting occasionally with the marinade, until the prawns have turned pink and lightly charred or the fish is opaque (has lost its translucency) and lightly charred. Serve immediately.

Makes 4–6

This is my version of a classic American recipe. If you prefer, you can use a fillet of beef to replace the rib-eye.

Serves 6

Make a spice mix by grinding the dried thyme, basil, cayenne, paprika, salt, onion seeds and English mustard powder together in a spice mill or pestle and mortar

Using a pastry brush, cover the beef in a thin film of Dijon mustard and then roll it in the spice mix so that it is well covered. Cover with clingfilm and leave to marinate in a cool place for at least 4 hours, or if possible overnight in the fridge. Allow 1 hour for the beef to come to room temperature before cooking, then remove the clingfilm.

Oil the barbecue grill and sear the beef on all sides over medium-hot coals (about 10 minutes); be careful as the spices might make your eyes water!

Transfer the beef to a baking tray. Cover with the barbecue lid if you have one and cook for about 30 minutes for rare meat, 45 minutes for medium-rare, turning and basting with the stock and wine from time to time. Leave to rest for 10–15 minutes before carving.

Cut the beef into 1cm-thick slices and serve with horseradish cream (see page 139) and the meat juices.

1.3kg piece of rib-eye beef, trimmed of all fat and sinew

2–3 tablespoons Dijon mustard

150ml beef stock

150ml red wine

For the spice mix:

2 teaspoons dried thyme

2 teaspoons dried basil

1 teaspoon cayenne pepper

2 teaspoons paprika

2 teaspoons salt

1 teaspoon onion seeds (kalonji)

1 teaspoon English mustard powder

I had these steaks served alongside slices of griddled pineapple and potato wedges and to my surprise, the sweet taste of the pineapple perfectly complemented the fragrant spice mix.

Serves 4

Put all the marinade ingredients in a food-processor and blend until they form a paste. Season with salt and pepper. Spread 2 tablespoons of the paste over each steak, coating both sides, and set aside the remainder of the paste. Cover the steaks with clingfilm and place them in the fridge to marinate for at least 4 hours, ideally overnight.

Remove the steaks from the fridge at least 30 minutes before you want to cook them. Barbecue the steaks over a fierce heat; for medium-rare, cook for 3–4 minutes, turning once. Allow to rest for 5 minutes on a warm plate.

While the steaks are 'resting', heat the reserved paste, adding water to your preferred sauce consistency. Serve as a sauce with the steaks.

4 rib-eye steaks, 250–300g each

For the marinade:

4 hot red chillies, deseeded and roughly chopped

2 tablespoons ground allspice (Jamaican pepper)

½ teaspoon ground cinnamon

⅛ teaspoon ground nutmeg

1½ teaspoons smoked paprika

6 spring onions, chopped

4 garlic cloves, sliced

2 tablespoons white wine vinegar

4 tablespoons extra virgin olive oil

chargrilled squid

1kg prepared squid, thoroughly cleaned and dried on a clean tea towel

6 tablespoons extra virgin olive oil

2 teaspoons crushed dried chilli flakes

4 garlic cloves, crushed to a paste with a little salt

2 teaspoons finely chopped oregano

It's best to use small but not tiny squid for this recipe. Squid needs a very short cooking time over hot coals otherwise it will become tough. It's great served with chilli sauce or chilli mayonnaise (page 141) and lime wedges.

Slit each squid body along one side and, with a sharp knife, score the inside of the body in a criss-cross pattern, ensuring you do not cut all the way through the flesh.

Combine the oil, chilli flakes, garlic and oregano in a bowl and toss in the squid. Cover and leave to marinate in the fridge for at least 1 hour, or for up to 24 hours. Allow to come to room temperature for about 30 minutes before cooking.

Set the squid pieces on the barbecue grill over very hot coals and chargrill each side for about 45 seconds, until white and no longer translucent. Serve at once.

Serves 4–6

herbed trout

4 whole trout, gutted and cleaned, heads removed if preferred

8 sprigs of rosemary

8 sprigs of fennel top (or use fresh dill sprigs)

8 sprigs of parsley

8 sprigs of oregano

100ml extra virgin olive oil

2 tablespoons lemon juice

salt and freshly ground black pepper

4 small heads fennel bulb

I can't recommend enough those specially designed hinged metal racks in the shape of small whole fish – they make turning fish so much easier and look fab on the barbecue.

Set the trout in a single layer in a shallow dish. Place two sprigs of each herb inside each trout and secure with wooden cocktail sticks. Pour over the oil and lemon juice and season with salt and pepper. Cover and leave to marinate in the fridge for at least 30 minutes or up to 8 hours.

Meanwhile, trim and halve the fennel and blanch in boiling salted water for 10 minutes. Drain and refresh in cold water, then place next to the trout and leave to marinate. Turn the fish and fennel occasionally, if possible.

Cook the trout, preferably in a hinged metal rack, and the fennel on the barbecue grill over medium-hot coals for about 15 minutes, turning occasionally, until the skin of the fish is lightly charred and the flesh is firm to the touch. Serve at once.

Serves 4

on the rack

swordfish in a citrus sauce

4 swordfish steaks, each weighing about 175g

For the marinade:

1 tablespoon vegetable oil, plus extra for greasing

1 garlic clove, finely chopped

1 small onion, finely chopped

¼ teaspoon crushed dried chillies

1 red chilli, deseeded and finely chopped

250ml fresh orange juice

50g golden caster sugar

100 ml fresh lime juice (about 3 limes)

1 tablespoon chopped coriander

½ teaspoon salt

Do not marinate for longer than 30 minutes otherwise the delicate flavour of the fish will be lost.

For the marinade, heat the oil in a saucepan over a medium heat, then add the garlic, onion, dried chillies and chopped chillies and cook for about 5 minutes or until the onion is softened, but not browned.

Stir in the remaining ingredients and bring to the boil, then reduce the heat to low and cook for a further 2 minutes. Transfer half the marinade to a bowl and allow to cool.

Once the marinade is cold, pour one half over the fish, and leave to marinate for 30 minutes.

Cook the remaining marinade over high heat for a further 8–10 minutes, or until thickened to a sauce consistency.

To cook the fish, brush the barbecue grill with oil and cook the steaks on the hottest part of the grill for 1–2 minutes each side, depending on how you like your fish cooked. Serve with the sauce.

This is an excellent way of spicing up a very good barbecue fish. The spice mixture can be made in advance and stored in an airtight continer in a cool, dark place for up to 3 months. Mackerel fillets need to be cooked over hot coals for only a short length of time.

To make the spice paste, heat a dry frying pan over a medium heat, then add the seeds and peppercorns and toast, shaking from time to time, for 2–3 minutes until the mustard seeds are popping and the spices are aromatic. (You may need to cover the frying pan to stop the mustard seeds jumping.) Blend the toasted spices with the chilli to a smooth powder in a coffee grinder or with a pestle and mortar. Combine the powder with salt and the brown sugar. Store in an airtight container until needed.

Half an hour before cooking the fish, lightly sprinkle both sides of each mackerel fillet with the spice mixture – about 2 teaspoons per fillet. Store any remaining spice mixture for future use.

For ease of turning, place the fillets in a metal hinged rack and cook on a hot barbecue for 1–2 minutes each side until lightly charred and firm to the touch. Delicious with cucumber sauce (page 135).

Serves 4–8

8 mackerel fillets, weighing about 100g each

For the spice paste:

1 tablespoon coriander seeds

1 tablespoon black mustard seeds

1 tablespoon cumin seeds

1 teaspoon black peppercorns

1 hot dried chilli, roughly chopped, deseeded if wished

1 teaspoon salt

1 tablespoon unrefined soft dark brown sugar

This recipe is not for the faint-hearted. It is best to grill lobster from raw so when preparing at home I follow RSPCA recommendations and put the live lobster in the freezer for 2 hours. I then split it in half with a sharp knife, first cutting along the natural line on the top of the head and then turning and cutting through the tail.

If you live close to a good fishmonger then ask him to do this for you as close to the time of cooking as possible. Store in the fridge. Remove the sac in the head space and the intestinal tract which runs along the length of the body before cooking.

To make the salsa, chop the herbs and combine with the remaining ingredients. You can stir in up to 4 tablespoons of cold water to thin the salsa, if preferred.

Remove the lobster halves from the fridge at least 30 minutes before cooking. Brush the cut surface of each half with melted butter and season lightly. Set them on the barbecue grill, shell-side down, and cover with the lid, if you have one, to cook for about 10 minutes. Turn and sear quickly on the cut surface, if wished. Serve at once, with the coriander salsa.

Serves 4

2 x 900g live lobsters

melted butter

salt and freshly ground black pepper

For the salsa:

50g coriander leaves

15g flat-leaf parsley leaves

3 spring onions, finely chopped

1 garlic clove, finely chopped

2 green chillies, deseeded and finely chopped

finely grated zest and juice of 1 lime

marinated salmon steaks

If you are using pre-soaked wood chips or other flavourings, sprinkle them over the hot coals or lava rocks before setting the fish on the barbecue to give the salmon a really smoky taste. Serve with grilled fennel and asparagus.

Combine all the marinade ingredients in a bowl. Place the fish in a dish and pour the marinade over. Cover and refrigerate for at least 30 minutes or up to 8 hours, then leave to stand at room temperature for a further 30 minutes before cookng.

Oil the barbecue grill and cook the salmon over hot coals, basting with the marinade, for about 5 minutes each side until lightly charred. Serve at once.

Serves 4

4 salmon steaks, or pieces of fillet, cut about 3cm thick

For the marinade:

2 tablespoons dry white wine

3 tablespoons light soy sauce

1 tablespoon unrefined light brown sugar

½ small onion, grated

1 small garlic clove, crushed

a dash of hot pepper sauce

¼ teaspoon freshly ground black pepper

peppered salmon with garlic & herb butter

It's best to make the butter at least a day in advance to allow the flavours to develop. It will keep for up to a week in the fridge, or three months in the freezer.

For the garlic and herb butter, beat the ingredients together in a small bowl until smooth. Cover and chill or transfer to a sheet of cling film or kitchen foil and roll into a log about 3cm in diameter. Chill or freeze until required.

Brush the salmon fillets lightly with oil, then sprinkle with salt. Press the crushed peppercorns over the surface. If you have time, cover and refrigerate for up to 24 hours, removing from the fridge at least 30 minutes before you want to cook them.

Cook on the grill rack of the barbecue over medium-hot coals, flesh-side down, for 4–5 minutes then turn and cook for a further 4–5 minutes, or until the salmon is cooked through and the skin is charred and crispy. Serve at once with the garlic and herb butter.

Serves 4

4 pieces of salmon fillets, weighing about 175g each

olive oil, for brushing

2 tablespoons mixed peppercorns (black, white, pink and green), crushed

salt

For the garlic and herb butter:

1 garlic clove, finely chopped

2 tablespoons chopped fresh mixed herbs (dill, tarragon, chives, parsley)

125g unsalted butter, at room temperature, diced

chargrilled butterflied prawns

16 jumbo raw prawns, shell on, heads removed

finely grated zest and juice of 2 limes

2 large red chillies, deseeded and finely diced

2 teaspoons grated fresh ginger

4 garlic cloves, finely chopped

4 tablespoons extra virgin olive oil

salt and freshly ground black pepper

Serves 4

Jumbo prawns are ideal for barbecuing, but remember to buy them with the shell on. Succulent, sweet and slightly spicy, this is a really simple recipe – the hardest part is shelling them!

Cut the prawns along the back. Turn them over, open them out and press flat. Remove the intestinal tract. The prawns are now 'butterflied'.

Arrange the prawns cut-side up on a tray, and sprinkle with the lime zest and juice, chilli, ginger, garlic, and some salt and pepper. Drizzle with the oil, cover and allow to marinate in the fridge for 30 minutes. Remove from the fridge 30 minutes before cooking.

Cook on a hot barbecue grill for 2–3 minutes shell-side down (in a rack, if you have one) until the shells are deep pink in colour, then turn and cook on the flesh side for 30 seconds. Serve at once.

monkfish with chermoula

4 fillets of prepared monkfish, 175–200g each

For the marinade:

2 garlic cloves, crushed

1 teaspoons ground cumin

½ teaspoon paprika

1 green chilli, deseeded and finely chopped

a small handful of coriander leaves, finely chopped

4 tablespoons lemon juice

4 tablespoons olive oil

salt

Serves 4

Monkfish is a firm white fish, ideal for barbecuing, especially when combined with chermoula – a Moroccan spicy paste that is perfect for marinating fish.

Mix together all the marinade ingredients, seasoning generously with salt, and pour half over the monkfish. Cover and refrigerate for 3–4 hours, turning occasionally. Remove from the fridge at least 30 minutes before cooking.

Barbecue the monkfish over hot coals for about 5 minutes on each side, basting with the coriander mixture, until lightly charred and just firm to the touch.

Spoon some of the reserved marinade over and serve at once.

on the rack

spatchcocked quail with coconut

8 quail, spatchcocked (see page 40)

1 teaspoon coriander seeds

1 teaspoon green cardamom pods, use the seeds only

2 teaspoons chopped garlic

1 teaspoon grated ginger

50g unsalted butter, melted

1 tablespoon vegetable oil

2 tablespoons chopped spring onion

1½ teaspoons ground cumin

1 teaspoon chopped coriander

3 tablespoons desiccated coconut

1 teaspoon unrefined soft brown sugar

Serves 4

Quail is the perfect 'vehicle' for these Indian flavours, and as a small bird, perfect for the barbecue. Double the amount of coconut mixture, if you wish, for a stronger taste.

With a pestle and mortar, grind the coriander seeds and 1 teaspoon salt with the seeds from the cardamom pods, then stir 1 teaspoon of the garlic, the ginger and the melted butter.

Smear the quails with the spiced butter mixture, cover and leave for at least 1 hour in a cool place, or overnight in the fridge. Remove from the fridge at least 30 minutes before cooking.

Heat the vegetable oil in a small saucepan and add the remaining 1 teaspoon garlic, the spring onion, cumin, coriander, desiccated coconut, sugar and 1 teaspoon pepper. Cook over medium heat until the coconut is golden, then set aside.

Set the quails, skin-side down, on an oiled barbecue grill over medium-hot coals and cook for 5–7 minutes until the skin is crispy. Turn and cook for a further 5–7 minutes until thoroughly cooked. Serve sprinkled with the coconut mixture.

barbecued duck

4–6 duck breasts

300ml American barbecue sauce, puréed until smooth (page 134)

Serves 4–6

Cooking the duck breasts in a tray first releases some of the fat from the skin – if cooked directly on the barbecue the fat would drip onto the coals causing large flames.

Set a metal baking tray on the barbecue grill over hot coals.

With a sharp knife, score the skin of each duck breast in a criss-cross pattern. When the tray is hot add the duck breasts skin-side down and sear them for about 10 minutes to release some of the fat. Turn and sear quickly on the other side. Remove from the baking tray and reserve the duck fat for another use.

Pat the excess fat from the duck breasts with kitchen paper then baste them with some of the barbecue sauce and cook skin-side down for about 5 minutes. Turn and brush them with the remaining sauce and cook for a further 5 minutes, or more depending on how you like your duck cooked, until crispy on the outside and pink to well-done in the centre.

Allow to rest for 5 minutes before serving. Meanwhile, thin any remaining sauce with a little water and simmer until heated through. Serve with the duck breasts.

You will need to start this recipe at least 24 hours in advance. If preferred, buy duck breasts with the skin removed, or remove it yourself, then there is no need to brown the duck breasts in the tray to release some of the fat, thus reducing cooking time to 10–15 minutes.

To make the marinade, heat the olive oil in a large pan over a medium heat, then cook the garlic, ginger and carrot together for 5 minutes, stirring frequently so they do not brown. Add the wine, 150ml water, the oregano, chilli, soy sauce, red pepper and honey and simmer for 10 minutes. Add the spring onions and cook for a further 5 minutes. Leave to cool completely.

Slash the duck breasts skin in a criss-cross fashion with a sharp knife. Set them in a single layer in a dish and pour over the cold marinade. Cover and marinate in the fridge for 24 hours before cooking.

To prepare the mushrooms, heat the olive and sesame oils in a large frying pan over a medium heat. Add the chilli and garlic and cook until softened but not browned. Meanwhile, arrange the mushrooms in a shallow dish.

Add the soy sauce and wine to the pan and boil quickly for 2 minutes. Remove from the heat and stir in the honey. Add the coriander, mint and season to taste. Pour this over the mushrooms, cover and marinate in the fridge for 2 hours, or preferably overnight.

Take the duck breasts out of the fridge about 30 minutes before cooking. Remove from the marinade and place skin-side down on a preheated baking tray, then cook on the barbecue grill for about 10 minutes. Discard the fat.

Transfer the duck breasts directly to the medium-hot coals on the barbecue grill and continue to cook them skin-side down until the skin is crispy – about 5 minutes. Turn them over and cook for a further 5–7 minutes. Paint the duck breasts with the marinade during cooking.

Allow the duck breast to rest for 5 minutes before serving. Meanwhile, bring the marinade to the boil then simmer for 5 minutes. Serve a little with the duck breasts.

Cook the mushrooms on medium-hot coals for about 3–5 minutes each side, basting from time to time with their marinade. Serve with the duck.

Serves 4

marinated duck with mushrooms

4 duck breasts

For the marinade:

100ml extra virgin olive oil

2 garlic cloves, finely diced

1 tablespoon diced ginger

1 carrot, finely diced

100ml dry white wine

1 tablespoon dried oregano

1 red chilli, deseeded and finely diced

2 tablespoons soy sauce

1 roasted red pepper, skinned, deseeded and diced

2 tablespoons clear honey

half a bunch spring onions, finely diced

For the mushrooms:

8 large cap mushrooms, stalks removed

6 tablespoons extra virgin olive oil

1 tablespoon toasted sesame oil

1 teaspoon finely chopped red chilli

2 garlic cloves, finely chopped

2 teaspoons soy sauce

2 tablespoons dry white wine

1 tablespoon clear honey

2 tablespoons chopped coriander

2 tablespoons chopped mint

salt and freshly ground black pepper

venison in port marinade

4 venison steaks

For the marinade:

100ml red wine

4 tablespoons ruby port

2 tablespoons red wine vinegar

3 tablespoons vegetable oil

2 garlic cloves, chopped

1 onion, chopped

1 carrot, chopped

1 celery stalk, chopped

a few sprigs of thyme

2 bay leaves

½ teaspoon black peppercorns, roughly crushed

Venison steaks are now available in the supermarkets and are a good alternative to beef steaks. Port is a traditional partner for venison, so why not use it on the barbecue too?

Combine all the marinade ingredients in a shallow dish. Turn the venison steaks in the marinade, then cover and leave in the fridge to marinate for at least 4 hours, preferably up to 24 hours. Remove from the fridge at least 30 minutes before cooking to bring back to room temperature.

Drain and pat dry with kitchen paper. Brush the venison steaks lightly with vegetable oil and oil the barbecue grill, then cook over high heat. For pink, cook for 2–3 minutes each side, for medium to well cooked 3–5 minutes each side. Season with salt then leave to rest for 5 minutes before serving.

indian spicy chicken

6 skinless and boneless chicken breasts

For the marinade:

4 garlic cloves, crushed with a little salt

300ml Greek-style yogurt

1 tablespoon grated onion

1 green chilli, deseeded and finely diced

1 teaspoon ground coriander

1 teaspoon ground turmeric

1 teaspoon chilli powder

1 teaspoon garam masala spice mix

½ teaspoon English mustard powder

Yogurt tenderises the chicken and beating the meat ensures that it won't take too long to cook. If there's any leftovers, the chicken makes a great sandwich filling with salad.

Mix together all the marinade ingredients.

Lay a chicken breast between two sheets of clingfilm, then beat it with a meat mallet or rolling pin until it's widened to about twice the size. Repeat with the remaining pieces of chicken. Cover the chicken with the yogurt mixture and marinate, covered, in the fridge for at least 2 hours or preferably overnight.

Remove from the fridge about 30 minutes before cooking. Wipe the excess yogurt from the chicken and oil the barbecue grill. Cook the chicken over hot coals for 4–5 minutes each side, until lightly charred.

This is a traditional recipe from Jamaica that I came across when I was over there. Take care with the Scotch bonnet chillies as they are really hot – and remove the seeds if you want to reduce the 'heat' a little.

Serves 6

To prepare the marinade, dry-fry the allspice 'berries' until they start to release their aroma and become crisp. Remove from the heat and blend to a fine powder in a coffee grinder or with a pestle and mortar.

Transfer the allspice powder to a food-processor along with all the remaining marinade ingredients, seasoning with about 1 teaspoon each of salt and pepper, and blend together.

Pour the marinade mixture onto the poussin, cover and leave in a cool place to marinate for about 2 hours, or preferably overnight in the fridge. Remove the poussin from the fridge about 1 hour before cooking.

Place the birds skin-side down on the barbecue grill over medium-hot coals and cook for about 15 minutes on each side, turning them frequently to prevent them from charring.

6 poussins, spatchcocked (see 40)

For the marinade:

2 teaspoons whole allspice (Jamaican pepper)

½ teaspoon ground nutmeg

½ teaspoon ground mace

1 teaspoon golden caster sugar

2 teaspoons dried thyme

175g spring onions, finely chopped

2 onions, finely chopped

2 Scotch bonnet chillies, deseeded if preferred for less heat

6 garlic cloves, finely chopped

2 tablespoons vegetable oil

salt and freshly ground black pepper

For a traditional presentation, serve these with noodles combined with some wilted spinach leaves and flavoured with chopped garlic, fresh ginger and light soy sauce.

In a shallow dish combine the soy, mirin or dry sherry, chilli sauce, sugar, ginger and garlic. Add the chicken thighs and turn them to coat with the marinade, then cover and refrigerate for at least 2 and up to 24 hours, turning from time to time. Remove from the fridge about 1 hour before cooking.

Cook the chicken thighs on the barbecue grill over hot coals for 8–10 minutes on each side, basting with the marinade several times during the cooking. Serve immediately.

For a grilled teriyaki tuna variation, take 4 tuna steaks, each about 2.5cm thick, marinate as above and cook on the oiled barbecue grill over hot coals for 2 minutes each side. Serve at once.

Serves 4

oriental chicken thighs

12 skinless and boneless chicken thighs

For the marinade:

5 tablespoons dark soy sauce

3 tablespoons mirin or dry sherry

3 tablespoons sweet chilli sauce

3 tablespoons unrefined soft brown sugar

2 tablespoons grated fresh ginger

2 garlic cloves, finely chopped

You do have to be careful about barbecuing chicken as it must be cooked properly, but chicken breasts generally cook quite evenly – do check every one before serving though.

In a small bowl, combine all the ingredients for the marinade mixture. Set the chicken breasts in a shallow dish and spread the mixture over them. Cover and marinate in the fridge for at least 2 hours, preferably overnight. Remove from the fridge up to 30 minutes before cooking.

Cook the chicken on the barbecue grill, skin-side down first, over high heat for 7–8 minutes. Then turn and cook on the other side for a further 7–8 minutes, basting occasionally with the marinade juices, until lightly charred and firm to the touch.

Serves 4

barbecue gingered chicken

4 chicken breasts with skin on, if preferred

For the marinade:

5cm piece fresh ginger, peeled and grated

1 small onion, grated

1 large red chilli, deseeded and finely chopped

2 garlic cloves, crushed with a little salt

1 tablespoon soy sauce

2 tablespoons vegetable oil

2 tablespoons clear honey

whole roast chicken with herbs

1 organic chicken (about 1.5kg)

lemon wedges, to serve

For the marinade:

1 tablespoon fennel seeds, toasted in a dry frying pan then crushed

3 garlic cloves, crushed with a little salt

1 tablespoon chopped rosemary leaves

1 tablespoon chopped thyme leaves

2 tablespoons olive oil

4 tablespoons lemon juice

salt and freshly ground black pepper

Serves 4

If you want to roast a chicken in a kettle barbecue, do make sure that you put plenty of charcoal in the barbecue to start with – or keep topping it up with pre-heated charcoal. It is essential that there is enough heat to keep the chicken cooking for 1¼–1½ hours and if you are unsure whether it is cooked through, it's best to use a meat probe to test the internal temperature of the cooked meat (it should be 75°C when inserted into the thickest part of the thigh).

Wash the bird inside and out and dry on kitchen paper. Set in a small roasting tin.

Mix all the ingredients for the marinade and spoon over and inside the bird. Cover and leave in the fridge for up to 24 hours. Remove from the fridge at least 1 hour before cooking.

Spoon the marinade juices over the chicken once more, then set the roasting tin on the grill of the barbecue. Close the lid and cook for 1¼–1½ hours until golden brown and cooked through. Allow to rest for 10–15 minutes, then serve with extra lemon wedges to squeeze.

lamb cutlets

4 x 3–4-cutlet racks of lamb

For the marinade:

1 tablespoon tomato paste

1 tablespoon harissa paste

3 tablespoons olive oil

2 garlic cloves, crushed with a little salt

freshly ground black pepper

Serves 4

Lamb racks are used in this recipe, but you could simply allow 12–16 cutlets for 4 people, marinated as below and seared on a hot barbecue for about 1 minute each side. Serve with skordalia (page 140) and a crisp green salad.

Combine all the marinade ingredients in a bowl, and season with a dash of pepper. Set the lamb racks in a shallow dish and brush them with the marinade. Cover and leave to marinate in the fridge for at least 1 hour, or overnight if possible.

Heat a baking tray on the barbecue grill until very hot. Place the lamb racks, fat-side down, in the tray for about 5 minutes or until the fat is crispy. Turn and sear on the other side for 5 minutes. Put the lid down on the barbecue and cook for a further 10–20 minutes, depending on how well cooked you like your lamb.

Leave the lamb to rest in the tray for 10 minutes. Slice the racks into cutlets, and serve with skordalia and a green salad with fresh mint leaves or coriander leaves.

The traditional name for this dish is raan – and this recipe was given to me by Manju Malhi. It will take about 2 hours to cook, on the bone, in a covered barbecue. For a speedier version, butterfly the leg and reduce the cooking time to 35–45 minutes. Tadka raita is a seasoned yogurt.

Serves 6

Prick the lamb all over with a skewer.

Mix all the ingredients for the marinade and smear it thickly over the surface of the lamb. Set it on a plate and cover loosely with foil (the foil should not touch the yogurt). Refrigerate for at least 2 hours or up to 24 hours. Remove from the fridge at least 1 hour before cooking.

Set a roasting tin on the barbecue grill to heat up. Put the leg of lamb in the tin and cook with the lid down for 2–2¼ hours, checking and turning occasionally, until the meat is cooked. (Test with a meat probe or skewer – the juices will run pink for medium-cooked and clear for well cooked.).

Leave the meat to rest for 15 minutes before carving.

While the lamb is resting, make the seasoned yogurt. Whip the yogurt until it is creamy. Fold in the onion, tomato, green chilli and salt.

Heat the oil in a small frying pan, then add the mustard seeds and curry leaves. Be careful as the mustard seeds will pop when heated. Fry for a few seconds, then add the peanuts, if using. Fry for a minute, making sure the mixture doesn't burn.

When the mixture has cooled, gently stir it into the yogurt. Serve chilled with the lamb.

1 leg of lamb

For the marinade:

3 tablespoons vegetable oil

3 garlic cloves, crushed

250ml Greek-style natural yogurt

1 tablespoon garam masala

1 teaspoon grated fresh ginger

a pinch of saffron strands

½ teaspoon salt

¼ teaspoon chilli powder

For the tadka raita:

250ml natural unsweetened yogurt

1 small onion, thinly sliced

1 medium-sized tomato, finely chopped

1 green chilli, deseeded if wished, finely chopped

½ teaspoon salt

1 tablespoon vegetable oil

½ teaspoon black mustard seeds

4 fresh curry leaves

10 unsalted skinned peanuts (optional)

burgers & ribs

How to barbecue burgers

A good burger depends on its ingredients, so start with the best minced meat available – for preference I'd go for organic. Mix your chosen ingredients then shape the burgers and leave them, covered, in the fridge for at least 1 hour, or overnight, for the flavours to develop. Remove from the fridge about 30 minutes before cooking.

Brush with vegetable oil and cook the burgers for 3–5 minutes on each side, depending on their thickness, how you like them cooked, and what variety of meat they are made from. Beef and lamb can be eaten pink, poultry and pork should be well cooked.

Serve with the usual accompaniments of toasted burger buns, tomato ketchup, mustard, sliced pickled cucumbers, onion rings and salad leaves.

How to barbecue ribs

Ribs are best simmered in flavoured stock before being barbecued. The initial cooking process makes them tender and flavoursome, then barbecuing caramelises all the flavourings and ensures that the meat is heated through. Grill the ribs on the barbecue for 10 minutes on each side, basting with reserved cooking liquor, and turning occasionally.

Burgers are classic barbecue fare, but I always feel for the vegetarian guests, which is why I have included a couple of veggie burgers (see also page 73.) This one is a very tasty alternative to 'bubble and squeak'.

Preheat the oven to 190°C/375°F/gas mark 5.

Place the parsnips, carrots and celeriac in a roasting tin and sprinkle with the olive oil. Toss to combine and place on the hob over high heat until the oil is sizzling. Transfer to the oven and cook for 20 minutes, stirring from time to time.

Add the onion and thyme to the root vegetables and cook for a further 10 minutes. Sprinkle with the vinegar and season with salt and ground black pepper to taste; allow to cool.

Stir the vegetables into the mashed potato, season and mix well to disperse. This mixture can be refrigerated for up to 24 hours. Shape the mix into 4 'burgers'.

Brush lightly with oil and cook on the barbecue over medium coals for about 4 minutes each side until golden and heated through.

Makes 4

roast vegetable bubble 'burgers'

175g parsnips, peeled and cut into 1cm dice

175g carrots, peeled and cut into 1cm dice

175g celeriac, peeled and cut into 1cm dice

2 tablespoons olive oil, plus extra for brushing

1 onion, finely chopped

1 tablespoon soft thyme leaves

1 tablespoon sherry vinegar

500g floury potatoes, cooked and mashed

salt and freshly ground black pepper

The honey in these burgers means that they need to be cooked over medium-hot coals otherwise they will char too quickly on the outside before being cooked in the centre.

Put the honey in a small non-stick frying pan and warm gently. Add the fish sauce and stir to combine. Stir to combine then leave to cool.

Put the minced pork in a large bowl and add the honey syrup, spring onions, garlic, lemongrass, cornflour, mint and coriander. Mix thoroughly. Season with salt and pepper.

Form the mixture into 6–8 'burgers' with slightly wet hands and place on a tray lined with greaseproof paper. Cover and chill in the fridge until required, for up to 8 hours. Remove at least 30 minutes before cooking to allow to come to room temperature.

Brush each 'burger' lightly with sesame oil and set on the barbecue. Cook over medium hot coals for 5–8 minutes each side, larger ones may take up to 10 minutes each side, turning occasionally. Serve with oriental dipping sauce (page 136).

Makes 6–8

asian pork burgers

4 tablespoons clear honey

6 tablespoons fish sauce (nam pla)

900g lean minced pork

8 spring onions, finely chopped

2 teaspoons crushed garlic

4 teaspoons finely chopped lemongrass, tender inner part of the stalk only

2 teaspoons cornflour

2 tablespoons finely chopped mint

4 tablespoons finely chopped coriander

sesame oil, for brushing

salt and freshly ground black pepper

sausage & potato burgers with apple sauce

2 medium-sized floury
potatoes, grated

900g pork sausages, skins
removed, or sausagemeat

2 medium eggs

2 small onions, finely
chopped

2 garlic cloves, finely
chopped

1 tablespoon finely chopped
sage

6 tablespoons plain flour

4 tablespoons thinly sliced
spring onions

salt

For the dry rub:

1 teaspoon ground
coriander

¼ teaspoon ground nutmeg

¼ teaspoon ground ginger

salt and ground black
pepper

For the apple sauce:

250ml prepared apple
sauce

¼ teaspooon ground
nutmeg

⅛ teaspoon ground ginger

If you're thinking of having a breakfast/brunch barbecue then these will be perfect – in which case, forget the apple sauce and try them with a fried egg on top.

In a small bowl, combine the dry-rub ingredients, seasoning well with salt and 1 teaspoon pepper, and set aside. In another bowl, combine the apple sauce ingredients and set aside.

Put the grated potatoes on a clean tea towel, then twist the towel to wring it out, squeezing as much moisture as possible from the potatoes. Transfer to a medium bowl and mix in the sausagemeat and eggs, then add the onions, garlic, sage, flour and spring onions, and season with salt. Mix well until evenly combined.

Using your hands, form the mixture into 8 'burgers', then sprinkle with the dry rub.

Set the burgers on the barbecue over a medium heat and cook for 6–8 minutes each side, turning occasionally until cooked through. Serve the burgers hot, with the apple sauce.

awt's all-american burger

No barbecue book, or for that matter, barbecue, is complete without a classic beef burger. Cooking the onion first will give the burger a much better flavour and prevent the burger from going black.

In a small frying pan, melt the butter and gently fry the onion, garlic, oregano and cumin until the onion is translucent and softened. Allow to cool then transfer to a large bowl and mix with the minced beef, olive oil, parsley and chilli sauce. Work with your hands to create a blended mixture, but do not overwork it.

Form the mixture into 6 'burgers', and chargrill them on the barbecue – for medium rare, 4–5 minutes each side, 6-8 minutes each side for well-done.

Fill the buns with the burgers and garnishes of your choice.

To garnish, choose from torn lettuce leaves, thinly sliced onion rings, thinly sliced tomato, sliced pickled gherkins, tomato ketchup, mustard and mayonnaise.

Makes 6

15g unsalted butter

1 small onion, finely chopped

1 teaspoon finely chopped garlic

1 teaspoon dried oregano

½ teaspoon ground cumin

1kg finely minced lean beef

1 tablespoon extra virgin olive oil

2 tablespoons chopped flat-leaf parsley

1 teaspoon chilli sauce

6 soft white burger buns, split and lightly chargrilled

salt and freshly ground black pepper

spicy chickpea burgers

Another fab veggie burger. If you have a kettle barbecue, cook the burgers with the lid down for a light smoky flavour. Serve with natural yogurt instead of ketchup or mayo.

Heat the oil in a small frying pan over a gentle heat, and cook the chilli, ginger, onion, celery and garlic until softened but not browned – about 10 minutes. Leave to cool.

Place the onion mixture in a food-processor with the chickpeas and coriander and whizz to combine. Add the egg, chilli paste and 75g of the breadcrumbs and season lightly with salt and freshly ground black pepper. Whizz until thoroughly mixed. Cover and refrigerate for at least 1 hour, or overnight, until ready to cook. Check the consistency of the mixture and add the remaining breadcrumbs if necessary to give a firm mixture.

Shape the mixture into 6–8 'burgers', brush with olive oil and cook over medium-hot coals for 4–5 minutes each side until golden and heated through. Serve with natural yogurt.

Variation
Replace the chickpeas with kidney beans and the onion with red onion.

Makes 6–8

2 tablespoons extra virgin olive oil, plus extra for brushing

1 red chilli, deseeded and finely chopped

1 teaspoon grated ginger

1 small onion, finely chopped

1 celery stalk, finely chopped

2 garlic cloves, crushed to a paste with a little salt

1 x 400g tin of chickpeas, drained and rinsed

2 tablespoons chopped coriander

1 egg, beaten

1 tablespoon chilli paste

75–100g fresh breadcrumbs

fiery pork & prawn burgers

350g minced pork

350g shelled raw prawns, finely chopped

4 tablespoons chopped water chestnuts

6 tablespoons finely chopped spring onions

2 garlic cloves, finely chopped

1 red chilli, finely chopped

2 tablespoons chicken stock – you may need more or less depending on mixture

1 tablespoon light soy sauce

1 teaspoon toasted sesame oil

1 teaspoon golden caster sugar

½ tablespoon cornflour

2 tablespoons chopped fresh coriander

½ teaspoon chilli powder

salt

This is a more unusual burger, flavoured with lots of oriental ingredients such as water chestnuts and spring onions. Prepare these up to 8 hours in advance to allow the flavours to develop.

Combine all the ingredients in a large bowl. Beat well for about 1 minute – you'll notice that the mixture becomes firmer. Divide the mixture into 4–6 portions and with slightly wet hands shape each into a 'burger'. Place on a tray, cover and refrigerate for up to 8 hours. Remove the burgers from the fridge about 30 minutes before cooking to bring them back to room temperature.

Cook on the barbecue over medium heat for 6–7 minutes each side for small ones, 8–10 minutes each side for larger ones, turning occasionally, until tender and golden brown. Alternatively, heat a frying pan on the barbecue and fry them over medium heat.

peppered lamb burgers

900g lean minced lamb

6 tablespoons chopped mint

2–3 tablespoons black peppercorns, crushed

1 teaspoon salt

A really straightforward burger. Minced mutton, which has a stronger flavour than lamb, is a good variation – and of course, choose the best-quality meat available.

Mix the lamb with the mint and season with salt, then shape into 4–6 'burgers'. Lightly coat them all over with crushed pepper. Cover and refrigerate for up to 8 hours.

Remove from the fridge about 30 minutes before cooking. Set the 'burgers' on the barbecue over medium heat and cook for 5–7 minutes each side, turning occasionally, until lightly charred and cooked. Larger burgers may take 2–3 minutes longer each side, depending on how well cooked you prefer them. Serve with natural yogurt.

spiced lamb burgers

1kg lean minced lamb

2 tablespoons red wine vinegar

2 tablespoons Dijon mustard

2 garlic cloves, crushed

1 tablespoon finely chopped rosemary

salt and black pepper

salsa verde (see page 138), to serve

Makes 6

This is a more delicately flavoured lamb recipe than the one on the previous page. Serve on toasted sourdough bread with sliced tomatoes or salsa verde (see page 138).

Mix together the lamb, vinegar, mustard, garlic and rosemary in a large bowl, and season. Form the mixture into 6 'burgers' and use straight away or cover and chill until required – up to 24 hours. Remove from the fridge about 30 minutes before cooking.

Place the burgers on the barbecue and cook until they are medium-rare, about 5 minutes each side, turning occasionally. Cook for 6–8 minutes each side for well-done. Serve with the salsa verde.

inverted turkey cheeseburgers

1 head garlic

extra virgin olive oil

750g minced turkey (or chicken)

2 tablespoons Dijon mustard

50g freshly grated parmesan cheese

50g unsalted butter, softened

1 tablespoon snipped chives

2–4 teaspoons coarsely ground black pepper

4 burger buns

For the garnish:

baby gem lettuce leaves

sliced tomatoes

red onion rings

large sweet pickled cucumbers, sliced lengthways

Makes 4

Almost like a 'burger kiev' with a surprise parmesan, garlic and chive butter in the middle. Great on their own (without the accompaniments) with a salad.

Separate the garlic cloves but do not peel them. Put them in a small saucepan and just cover with olive oil. Cook gently for 8–10 minutes, until the garlic is golden and softened. Remove from the oil and allow to cool, and set aside the oil.

Push the garlic pulp out of each clove with the back of a knife. Place the garlic pulp in a bowl and drizzle with a little of the olive oil. In a large bowl, combine 1 tablespoon (or all if preferred) of the garlic pulp with the turkey and mustard and mix thoroughly.

In a separate dish, mash together the Parmesan, butter and chives. Set aside.

Form the turkey mixture into 4 patties. Divide the cheese butter into 4. Make a deep indentation in each patty and place one nugget of 'cheese butter' in each indentation, folding the turkey back around the cheese until it is completely sealed. Sprinkle some black pepper over each burger, cover and refrigerate for up to 8 hours. Remove from the fridge about 30 minutes before cooking.

Barbecue the patties over medium-hot coals for 10 minutes each side until cooked through. Season with salt. If using, split and chargrill the burger buns, then fill with the burgers and garnishes of your choice.

These ribs are much lighter in colour and flavour than the more traditional barbecue recipe on the following page, but they are equally sticky, fingerlickin' and unctuous.

Mix the dry rub ingredients in a small bowl and rub into the ribs. Place the ribs in a plastic container and refrigerate for at least 2 hours.

Meanwhile, in a heavy saucepan, combine the stock, brown sugar, dried and fresh ginger, chillies, rice wine, oyster sauce, onion, garlic, rice vinegar and salt. Over a medium-low heat, simmer the mixture for 15 minutes, add the ribs and cook over a gentle heat for 45 minutes covered.

Allow to cool, refrigerate, then remove the fat. Remove the ribs and strain the marinade. Place the marinade on a medium heat and cook until the liquid has reduced by half and is sticky. Allow to cool.

Remove the ribs from the fridge at least 30 minutes before cooking. Baste the ribs with the marinade and cook for 20–25 minutes on the barbecue, turning from time to time and painting with the marinade to build up a sticky glaze.

Serve with more sauce on the side.

sweetened spice ribs

1.2 litres chicken stock

75g soft dark brown sugar

2 tablespoons dried ginger

2.5cm fresh ginger, sliced

2 red chillies, sliced

4 garlic cloves, sliced

4 tablespoons Chinese rice wine

4 tablespoons oyster sauce

1 onion, finely sliced

1 teaspoon rice vinegar

½ teaspoon salt

For the dry rub:

4 tablespoons brown sugar

1 teaspoon dry mustard

1 teaspoon salt

½ teaspoon ground ginger

½ teaspoon ground cinnamon

4 baby back ribs

You can buy 'sheets' of spare ribs, which can be left whole or cut into manageable lengths for cooking, then cut into individual ribs once they have been barbecued. Serve with potato skins and chargrilled corn on the cobs, with napkins and finger bowls on hand for those sticky fingers.

Serves 6

Put all the marinade ingredients in a large shallow dish, then mix thoroughly to combine. Add the ribs and turn them in the mixture to coat evenly. Cover and leave to marinate in a cool place for 2–4 hours, or in the fridge for up to 24 hours.

Put the ribs in a large, deep saucepan – you may have to split the sheet in half to fit. Pour over the tomato ketchup mixture and add just enough water to cover the ribs completely. Bring to a simmer, then cover and cook over a medium heat for about 1 hour until completely tender. Remove the ribs from the heat and transfer to a large shallow non-metallic dish. Allow the ribs to cool in the marinade, then chill until ready to put on the barbecue. They can be kept in the fridge for up to 24 hours.

When ready to use the ribs, carefully scoop off the fat from the top of the mixture and discard, then allow the mixture to come back to room temperature. Drain off all the marinade and pour some into a large, wide saucepan. Cook it over medium heat, stirring occasionally, until reduced to a sticky coating consistency.

Set the ribs on the barbecue grill over medium-high heat and cook for 8–10 minutes each side, occasionally basting or painting the ribs with the reduced marinade until lightly charred.

To serve, cut into single ribs and arrange on a large platter.

fingerlicking ribs

3kg pork spare ribs

For the marinade:

300ml tomato ketchup

300ml soy sauce

125g clear honey

5cm piece fresh ginger, peeled and finely grated

4 garlic cloves, crushed

5 tablespoons dry sherry

1 teaspoon ground star anise

1 tablespoon chopped rosemary

skewers & sticks

About skewers and sticks

Chunks of meat, veg or fruit on a stick are another time-honoured way to cook food on a barbecue. They are also a great means of combining texture, flavour and including healthy vegetables with meat.

The recipes in this chapter will give you lots of ideas, but do feel free to create your own combination of ingredients – bearing in mind the shape and colour of the food (you can get quite absorbed in creating artistic schemes) as well as complementary flavours.

Skewers also look great and need very little help in presentation – just lay them on a platter and your guests can grab them and munch as they wander around. But they are also an easy way to cook food – for example, jumbo prawns (see page 46) because you can turn them all at once, rather than individually. You could also barbecue them in a hinged metal rack to make life really easy.

Types of skewer

A variety of metal and wooden or bamboo skewers is available. You can also use strong stems of rosemary with the leaves removed (see the lamb kofte on page 91)

Metal skewers are best for meat as they conduct heat.

You should always soak bamboo skewers in water for at least 30 minutes before threading. The idea is that the skewers absorb some water, and this will reduce the scorching of the sticks while they're on the barbecue grill, but I find that they still burn.

How to assemble and barbecue skewered food

Prepare evenly sized pieces of food – meat, fish, poultry and vegetables – and you can also barbecue fruit for a skewered dessert (see page 147). They may be marinated first – and in the case of vegetables it is sometimes better to blanch (root vegetables) or even pre-cook (whole new potatoes) them.

If you are using metal skewers, brush or smear them with oil and thread on the chosen ingredients, ensuring that you start and finish with a solid, chunky ingredient that will hold the others in place.

Cook over medium-high heat, turning the skewers frequently and basting as necessary. Fish and fruit will cook in about 5 minutes. Chunks of meat on a skewer will take 5–10 minutes depending on the variety, while flavoured minced meat pressed onto skewers may take 10–15 minutes, depending on the thickness and variety of the meat.

middle eastern minced lamb

1 medium onion, quartered

2 garlic cloves, roughly chopped

a small handful of parsley, roughly chopped

a small handful of coriander leaves, roughly chopped

½ teaspoon ground allspice

½ teaspoon ground cinnamon

½ teaspoon paprika

½ teaspoon cayenne pepper

600g minced lean lamb

extra virgin olive oil, for brushing

salt and ground black pepper

A great way to serve this is to grill some pitta bread and create a pocket by cutting through the side 'seam'. Place shredded lettuce, chopped onion and tomato, mint and coriander leaves in the pockets, top with a kebab (off the skewer!) and spoon a little Greek yogurt on top.

Soak 16 small bamboo skewers in cold water for 30 minutes. Put the onion, garlic, herbs, spices and salt and pepper to taste in a food-processor and blend to a coarse paste. Add the lamb and pulse just until the mixture is well combined.

Shape the mixture into 'sausages' about 8cm long and mould each sausage around a wooden skewer. Squeeze the meat tightly so it clings to the skewer. Cover and refrigerate for up to 8 hours, but remove from the fridge at least 30 minutes before cooking.

Place the kebabs on a hot, oiled barbecue grill and cook for 3–5 minutes each side until lightly charred and firm to the touch.

Makes 16

souvlakia

A classic Greek kebab, this is less spicy than the middle eastern skewer opposite, but is also great served off the skewer, in a pitta pocket with lots of lettuce and Greek yogurt.

Makes 4

Mix the oregano with the oil, lemon juice and onion in a bowl to make the marinade. Place the meat in the marinade and let it stand at room temperature for 1 hour, or preferably cover and refrigerate overnight. Drain away the marinade.

Thread the pieces of meat onto long metal skewers and place on the barbecue grill over hot coals, turning them occasionally, for 5–10 minutes, depending on how rare you like your lamb. It will be ready when nicely brown on the outside but still pink on the inside. Season and serve with salad.

1 tablespoon finely chopped oregano

3 tablespoons extra virgin olive oil

1 tablespoon lemon juice

1 tablespoon grated onion with its juice

500g lean lamb (from the leg) cut into 3cm pieces

salt and freshly ground black pepper

quick tandoori chicken skewers

Here's an Indian-style kebab that will turn a lovely warm colour on the barbecue. The yogurt will keep the chicken soft and tender, but remember to check that every skewer has cooked through before serving.

Makes 4

Mix the chicken with the lemon juice and salt in a bowl and set aside for about 20 minutes, turning the chicken occasionally during this time.

In a food-processor, combine the curry paste ingredients and blend to a smooth paste. Add the chicken, cover and refrigerate for at least 3 hours or preferably overnight. Remove the chicken from the fridge 30 minutes before cooking.

Take the chicken pieces from the bowl and shake off as much of the marinade as possible. Thread onto metal skewers. Place on a hot, oiled barbecue grill and cook for 8–10 minutes, turning occasionally, until the meat is lightly charred and white (no longer pink) when tested. Serve straight away with the lemon or lime wedges.

3 skinless and boneless chicken breasts, cut into 3cm chunks

1 tablespoon lemon juice

1 teaspoon salt

For the curry paste:

200g Greek-style yogurt

half an onion, grated

1 tablespoon grated fresh ginger

1 tablespoon crushed garlic

1 small green chilli, deseeded and finely chopped

2 teaspoons garam masala

2 tablespoons tandoori curry paste

lemon or lime wedges, to garnish

oriental pork and pineapple kebabs

This is one instance where sweet and savoury combine beautifully. The slightly sharp pineapple juice helps to cut through the richness of the oyster and soy sauces.

Makes 4

Combine the pork and the remaining ingredients, with the exception of the pineapple. Cover with clingfilm and allow to marinate for 3–4 hours in the fridge. Remove at least 30 minutes before cooking.

Meanwhile, soak 8 small bamboo skewers in cold water for 30 minutes. Thread alternate chunks of pineapple and pork onto the skewers.

Set the kebabs on the barbecue grill over medium-hot coals and chargrill for 10–12 minutes, turning them from time to time until the pork is cooked through. Brush the pork with any remaining marinade while it is cooking. Serve immediately.

500g pork fillet (tenderloin), cut into 24 chunks

1 tablespoon oyster sauce

1 tablespoon soy sauce

1 tablespoon rice wine vinegar

¼ teaspoon ground white pepper

1 tablespoon finely chopped red chilli

1 tablespoon grated ginger

1 shallot, finely chopped

24 chunks of fresh pineapple, cut the same size as the pork

fish kebabs with cucumber raita

You can use any white fish – pollack, seabass, haddock, whiting or cod. Leftover raita will keep in the fridge for 3–4 days and can be used as a dip or accompaniment to grilled chicken or salmon.

Makes 12

To make the fish kebabs, skin and chop the fish into chunks.

Whizz the white fish in a food-processor until finely minced. Transfer to a large mixing bowl and mix in the chopped salmon and lime zest. Add all the other kebab ingredients, season with salt and freshly ground black pepper, and mix well. Mould the fish mixture onto 12 skewers, forming 12 sausage-shaped kebabs, about 3cm in diameter. Cover and refrigerate for up to 8 hours, removing at least 30 minutes before cooking.

Cook the kebabs on the barbecue grill over medium-high heat for 3–4 minutes each side until firm to the touch and lightly charred. Serve immediately, with the cucumber raita (see page 135).

300g white fish fillet

300g salmon fillet

zest and juice of 1 lime

1 small fennel bulb, chopped

a small bunch of coriander, finely chopped

4–8 green chillies, deseeded and finely chopped

4 spring onions, chopped

2 tablespoons fennel seeds, finely ground

2 tablespoons coriander seeds, finely ground

2 tablespoons vegetable oil

1 tablespoon crushed garlic

1 tablespoon grated ginger

beef satay with chilli peanut sauce

600g lean rump steak, cut into 32 chunks

For the marinade:

8 shallots, finely chopped

6 garlic cloves, peeled, sliced

3 red chillies, deseeded, diced

2.5cm piece of ginger or galangal, peeled and sliced

2 teaspoons ground turmeric

2 teaspoons ground coriander

½ tablespoon chunky peanut butter

1 teaspoon shrimp paste

pinch of grated nutmeg

2 whole cloves

2 tablespoons vegetable oil

This marinade is so easy to make and can be used to flavour chicken and lamb too. The shrimp paste is optional here, but will make the marinade taste more authentic.

Whizz all the marinade ingredients except the oil in a food-processor, or pound with a mortar and pestle, to form a paste. Heat the oil in a frying pan and sauté the mixture for about 5 minutes, then allow to cool. Add the beef, cover and marinate in the fridge for at least 3 hours, or ideally overnight. Remove from the fridge 30 minutes before cooking.

Thread 4 cubes of beef onto each skewer. Grill on the barbecue over hot coals for 1–2 minutes each side, until browned and cooked to your liking. Serve immediately, with the chilli peanut sauce (see page 137).

parsnip & carrot skewers

8 large parsnips

8–12 large carrots

vegetable oil for brushing

For the lime butter:

1 spring onion, finely chopped

1 garlic clove, finely chopped

200g unsalted butter, diced

1 tablespoon finely chopped green chilli

1 teaspoon grated ginger

1 tablespoon fresh lime juice

2 teaspoons finely grated lime zest

For the lime butter, cook the spring onion and garlic with a knob of the butter until softened but not browned. Leave to go cold.

Beat the rest of the butter until smooth then beat in the remaining ingredients, together with half a teaspoon of salt and of pepper and the onion mixture. Alternatively, pulse in a food-processor until just mixed. Cover and leave to one side or transfer to a sheet of cling-film or kitchen foil and roll into a log about 3cm in diameter. Chill or freeze until required.

Peel and cut the vegetables into large even-sized chunks. Transfer to a large saucepan and just cover with cold water. Bring to the boil then simmer for 3–5 minutes until just tender enough to thread onto skewers. Drain and refresh in cold water.

Oil 8 metal skewers and thread the parsnip and carrot pieces alternately. Cover and leave to one side.

Brush the vegetable skewers lightly with oil and cook on the barbecue over medium-hot coals for about 10 minutes, turning frequently until lightly charred and tender. Serve at once with the lime butter.

Lamb, yogurt, coriander and mint are made for each other and a classic combination in middle-eastern and Indian cooking. Double the amount of sauce, if wished. The rosemary stems will give the kofte a fragrant aroma.

Soak the rosemary stems (if using) or bamboo skewers in cold water for 30 minutes or so to reduce scorching. Meanwhile, combine all the kofta ingredients in a bowl and mix thoroughly with your hands. Ideally, cover and leave the mixture in the fridge for about 1 hour, or up to 8 hours, for the flavours to develop. Remove 30 minutes before cooking.

Drain the skewers. Shape the mixture into 48 balls and thread them onto the chosen skewers. Cook over medium-hot coals on the barbecue, turning the skewers regularly until lightly charred – about 10 minutes.

Meanwhile, combine the yogurt sauce ingredients in a bowl. Serve the kofte with the sauce.

Makes 16

spiced lamb kofte

16 rosemary sprigs on long firm stems (optional)

For the kofte:

1kg finely minced lamb

1 small onion, coarsely grated

2cm piece of fresh ginger, peeled and grated

2 garlic cloves, crushed to a paste with salt

1 teaspoon ground coriander

2 teaspoons ground cumin

finely grated zest of 1 orange

1 teaspoon paprika

1 teaspoon ground cinnamon

½ teaspoon turmeric

½ teaspoon chilli powder

2 tablespoons finely chopped parsley

2 tablespoons finely chopped coriander leaves

1 egg

salt and freshly ground black pepper

For the yogurt sauce:

200ml thick Greek-style yogurt

1 tablespoon chopped coriander leaves

1 tablespoon chopped mint

feta kebabs

16 baby new potatoes, scrubbed

2 garlic cloves, cut into slivers

400g feta cheese

16 button mushrooms

16 cherry tomatoes

8–16 fresh bay leaves

vegetable oil, for brushing

baby gem lettuce leaves, washed and dried

salt and freshly ground pepper

chilli peanut sauce (see page 137), to serve

Makes 8

I serve this with chilli peanut sauce (see the recipe on page 137), but adding 6 garlic cloves and a small bunch of coriander leaves, all whizzed in a food-processor until finely chopped, and then 1 tablespoon dry sherry.

Put the potatoes into a saucepan of boiling salted water. Bring back to the boil and cook for 15–20 minutes until just tender. Drain and leave to cool completely.

With the tip of a sharp knife, make incisions in the potatoes and insert some slivers of garlic into each one.

Cut the feta cheese into sixteen evenly sized pieces. Thread the garlic potatoes, cheese, mushrooms, cherry tomatoes and bay leaves onto 8 skewers. Brush with oil and season well. Cover and refrigerate for up to 24 hours.

Barbecue the kebabs over a medium heat for 8–10 minutes, turning occasionally, until the vegetables are tender and the cheese is golden. Serve the kebabs with the warm, spicy chilli peanut sauce and baby gem lettuce leaves.

moroccan monkfish kebabs

700g fillets trimmed monkfish, cut into 4cm chunks

For the marinade:

150ml olive oil

2 tablespoons chopped coriander

1 tablespoon chopped mint

4 garlic cloves, crushed to a paste with a little salt

juice of 1 lemon

½ teaspoon chilli powder

½ teaspoon paprika

2 teaspoons ground cumin

1 teaspoon ground coriander

½ teaspoon ground black pepper

Makes 4–6

This firm fish can take these wonderful flavours. Putting the kebabs inside a hinged metal rack makes them much easier to turn – and also reduces the chance of the fish falling off the skewers!

Mix together all the marinade ingredients and season with a pinch of salt, and pour it over the monkfish. Cover and refrigerate for 3–4 hours, turning occasionally.

Remove from the fridge about 30 minutes before cooking. Thread the monkfish onto skewers. Place in a hinged fish rack and cook on a hot barbecue for 3–4 minutes each side, basting with the marinade, until the fish is just firm to the touch and lightly charred. Serve immediately.

Swordfish needs high heat and a short cooking time, so ensure the coals are hot before you put the kebabs on the barbecue. The pickled lemons and tomatoes will create a brightly coloured skewer.

Cut the pickled lemons in half, scoop out the flesh and discard. Cut 3 of the lemons in half and then half again to make 12 pieces of roughly even size.

Roughly chop the rind of the fourth lemon and put it in a food-processor with the marinade ingredients and 2 tablespoons of cold water and pulse until smooth. Transfer to a bowl and add the swordfish pieces. Leave to marinate in the fridge for 20–30 minutes.

Thread one piece of swordfish on to each of four long skewers. Follow the swordfish with one bay leaf, one tomato and one piece of lemon rind. Repeat, finishing each kebab with a piece of fish.

Cook on the barbecue over hot coals for 1–2 minutes each side until charred and the fish is firm to the touch. Serve with a leaf salad.

swordfish kebabs with pickled lemon

4 pickled lemons

800g–1kg swordfish fillets, cut into 16 even-sized cubes

12 bay leaves

12 cherry tomatoes

For the marinade:

a small bunch of mint, leaves only

4 garlic cloves, roughly chopped

½ teaspoon crushed dried chilli

2 tablespoons olive oil

marinated haloumi cheese kebabs

500g haloumi cheese, cut into 24 cubes

16 fresh bay leaves

1 red pepper, deseeded and cut into 16 pieces

2 small red onions, each cut into 8 wedges

16 x 3cm chunks of pumpkin, blanched

16 x 3cm chunks of courgette

For the marinade:

1 teaspoon chopped thyme

1 teaspoon chopped oregano

1 teaspoon chopped rosemary

1 teaspoon chopped mint

1 teaspoon chopped parsley

1 garlic clove, mashed to a paste with a little salt

1 green chilli, deseeded and finely chopped

5 tablespoons olive oil

finely grated zest and juice of 1 lime

½ teaspoon freshly ground black pepper

This is a veggie kebab with plenty of flavour. Haloumi is a great cooking cheese as it keeps its shape but browns and softens to give a crisp 'crust' and a chewy centre.

To make the marinade, combine all the marinade ingredients.

Put the cheese, bay leaves and vegetables in a large bowl and pour the marinade over them, mixing very thoroughly. Cover and place in the fridge for 2–4 hours, or up to 24 hours, turning occasionally to combine the flavours.

Thread eight metal skewers with the haloumi, bay leaves and vegetable chunks, starting and finishing with a piece of cheese.

Place the kebabs on the barbecue grill over hot coals, turning frequently until they are golden brown, about 8–10 minutes. Brush the kebabs lightly with any remaining marinade during cooking. Serve immediately.

veg out

How to chargrill vegetables

Most vegetables can be chargrilled on the barbecue – some from their raw state, but others need to be blanched or even fairly well cooked first.

To blanch or not to blanch?

In general, green and salad vegetables such as courgettes, asparagus, spring onions, fennel and peppers do not need to be blanched, but in some cases it does help to 'set' the bright green colour or start the cooking process.

Root vegetables such as onions, carrots, parsnips and potatoes are best part-cooked, otherwise they will take a very long time to cook on the barbecue, resulting in over-charred skins and crunchy centres. Other vegetables worth blanching or part-cooking are corn on the cob, pumpkin and squash.

Preparation essentials

Prepare your chosen vegetables by cutting them into halves, even slices or chunks. Blanch or part-cook as necessary, then refresh in iced water. Drain and dry on a clean tea-towel, and transfer to the marinade. Cover and leave to marinate for at least 1 hour or overnight in the fridge. Remove from the marinade and shake off the excess.

Cook the vegetables on the barbecue grill – thread them onto skewers if you prefer – over medium-hot coals until thoroughly cooked and nicely charred. The timing will depend on the type and size of the vegetables.

Serve the vegetables straight away, or return them to the marinade until required – they're good served warm or cold.

barbecued jacket potatoes

Choose evenly sized medium potatoes. Scrub well, then prick all over with a fork. Rub with oil then wrap each in a double thickness of kitchen foil. Bury the parcels in the embers of the barbecue, or set on the barbecue grill and put the lid down. Cook, turning occasionally, for about 45 minutes.

To speed up the cooking, start off the potatoes in a preheated oven at 200°C/400°F/gas mark 6 for 30 minutes, and then reduce the barbecue time to about 20 minutes.

portobello mushrooms with brie

This is a simple recipe with lots of flavour. The mushrooms stay wonderfully moist, especially with the cheese topping. If you don't have a kettle barbecue, just cover the mushrooms with foil or a domed saucepan lid.

Wipe the mushrooms and discard the stalks. Mix the oil with the garlic and thyme and season with pepper. Brush the caps of the mushrooms with the oil mixture and leave for 1 hour or up to 24 hours in the fridge to allow the flavours to develop.

Set the mushrooms gill-side down on the barbecue grill and cook over medium-hot coals for 4–6 minutes, turning occasionally until tender and lightly charred. Set the mushrooms gill-side up and cover each with a slice of brie. Cover with the lid, or loosely with foil or a domed saucepan lid, and cook for a further 1–2 minutes, until the cheese has started to melt. Serve at once.

Serves 4–8

8 large portobello mushrooms

4 tablespoons olive oil

2 garlic cloves, crushed with a little salt

1 tablespoon thyme leaves

250g brie cheese, sliced

freshly ground black pepper

dressing for barbecued vegetables

This is a multi-purpose dressing for any chargrilled veg, whether you are cooking peppers on the barbie or making up skewers. Feel free to add more or less herbs and spices to your taste.

Combine all the ingredients in a large bowl or dish. Use as described in Preparation Essentials (see left).

1 shallot, peeled and diced

1 red chilli, deseeded and finely diced

3 garlic cloves, peeled and diced

6 basil leaves, ripped

1 tablespoon chopped oregano

8 tablespoons olive oil

4 anchovy fillets, finely chopped (optional)

2 tablespoons sherry vinegar

salt and freshly ground black pepper

roast tomatoes stuffed with garlic ricotta

4 ripe beefsteak tomatoes
or 8 large tomatoes

For the garlic ricotta:

1 garlic head

1 teaspoon extra virgin
olive oil

250g ricotta cheese

1 tablespoon snipped
chives

½ teaspoon salt

¼ teaspoon freshly ground
black pepper

Garlic ricotta is also good served as a simple appetiser with grissini (breadsticks) or crudités (chunks of raw vegetables). It will keep, covered and refrigerated, for up to three days.

For the garlic ricotta, cut 5mm off the pointed end of the head of garlic. Drizzle the exposed garlic with the olive oil. Wrap the garlic in a double thickness of kitchen foil and cook on the barbecue for 20–30 minutes, turning from time to time, until tender. (Alternatively, roast in the oven at 190°C/375°F/gas mark 5 for 35–40 minutes.)

Allow the garlic to cool a little before separating the cloves. Squeeze or push the cloves with the back of a knife so that the soft garlic pulp pops out of its skin.

Combine all the remaining ingredients with the roasted garlic pulp and mix until fairly smooth. Slice the tops off the tomatoes and set aside. Scoop out and discard the pulp and seeds from the middle of each tomato.

Stuff the tomatoes with the garlic ricotta. Replace the tops on the tomatoes and arrange them in a metal dish. Cook on the barbecue with the lid down (or cover loosely with foil or a domed saucepan lid) for 5–10 minutes, depending on size until the cheese is just starting to ooze from the tomatoes. Serve immediately.

barbecued corn cobs

4 corn cobs, husks removed

For the flavoured butter:

100g unsalted butter, diced

1 garlic clove, crushed with
a little salt

1 tablespoon clear honey

½ teaspoon chilli powder

1 teaspoon ground cumin

1 teaspoon ground coriander

1 teaspoon freshly ground
black pepper

Cook the corn cobs in boiling but not salted water (salt makes the kernels tougher) for 6–8 minutes before barbecuing, for a more tender result. You can also use frozen corn cobs instead of fresh, but defrost before cooking. Or roast them in their husks for 10–15 minutes until well charred, turning frequently, then peel back the husks and serve with the butter.

Put all the flavoured butter ingredients in a small saucepan and melt over a gentle heat. Stir to combine.

Brush the corn cobs with the flavoured butter and cook on the barbecue for about 10 minutes, turning regularly until golden. Baste frequently during cooking.

6 red peppers, halved and deseeded

75g salted capers, soaked and drained

3 garlic cloves, cut in slivers

1 tablespoon finely ripped basil

1 tablespoon roughly chopped oregano (or 1 teaspoon dried oregano)

2 tablespoons chopped flat-leaf parsley

2 tablespoons extra virgin olive oil

2 tablespoons balsamic vinegar

parmesan cheese shavings (optional)

freshly ground black pepper

chargrilled peppers with capers and herbs

Red peppers are best for this recipe as they have a delectable sweetness when cooked and their skins will look great when slightly blackened – you can peel off the blackened bits if you prefer.

Cook the peppers skin-side down on the barbecue until lightly charred all over and just tender – 10–15 minutes. Transfer to a serving dish.

Combine the capers, garlic and herbs and season with black pepper. Stir in the olive oil and balsamic vinegar. Spoon this over the peppers and serve topped with shavings of parmesan.

Serves 6–12

These skewers are best served as a side dish rather than eaten in one go, but will go well with lamb or beef dishes.

Makes 4

Place the onions in a wide saucepan with the garlic cloves and cover with cold water. Bring to the boil, then drain and refresh in cold water. Carefully cut each onion into 8 wedges, making sure that each piece is held in place by a section of the root.

Thread a garlic clove onto each of 4 metal skewers, then thread the onion wedges and secure with another garlic clove. Drizzle with the oil and sprinkle with the thyme, then season with salt and pepper. If you have time, cover and refrigerate for up to 24 hours.

Cook on the barbecue grill over medium-hot coals for 10–15 minutes, turning occasionally, until tender and lightly charred. Drizzle with balsamic vinegar before serving.

4 large red onions

8 garlic cloves

2 tablespoons extra virgin olive oil

leaves from 4 sprigs of thyme

salt and freshly ground black pepper

balsamic vinegar, to sprinkle

I love aubergines, especially when grilled with olive oil. This recipe is delicious served with a salad of rocket leaves and natural yogurt.

Serves 8

Cut the aubergines in half lengthways. With a sharp knife, score the surface of the cut flesh with criss-cross hatch marks. Brush the cut surfaces with the oil and season with a little salt and pepper. Cook over the direct heat of the barbecue over medium coals for 7–8 minutes on the flesh side, then 7–8 minutes on the skin side. Keep an eye on them and turn as necessary so that they don't burn. Remove the aubergines from the barbecue and allow to cool.

In a food-processor blend the remaining ingredients to a smooth paste. The mixture should be the thickness of double cream, so if necessary thin it down with a little boiling water. The recipe can be prepared ahead to this point.

Spread the cut surface of each aubergine half liberally with the nut paste and cook on the barbecue, skin-side down (close the lid if you have one or cover loosely with foil) over medium coals for about 5 minutes, just until the aubergines are heated through.

8 large aubergines

1 tablespoon olive oil

1 tablespoon chopped garlic

3 tablespoons chopped coriander leaves

175g crunchy peanut butter

2 tablespoons toasted sesame oil

5 tablespoons soy sauce

5 tablespoons unrefined dark Muscovado sugar

2 teaspoons rice wine vinegar

1 tablespoon chilli oil

salt and freshly ground black pepper

small aubergines in the embers

8 small aubergines, each weighing 100–125g

4 tablespoons extra virgin olive oil

juice of 1 lemon

4 anchovy fillets, chopped

2 tablespoons ripped fresh basil leaves

salt and freshly ground black pepper

Make sure the aubergines are thoroughly cooked and they will be delicious. An under-cooked aubergine is not a pleasant experience! As an alternative to the dressing in the recipe, try a fresh tomato salsa or tomato chutney.

Wrap each aubergine in a double thickness of kitchen foil and bury them in the embers of the barbecue. Cook for 15–20 minutes, turning occasionally until completely softened (test with a metal skewer – it should go through very easily), then remove the foil and set them on the barbecue grill. Cook just until lightly charred, turning the aubergines from time to time.

Combine the remaining ingredients to make a dressing.

Cut the aubergines open and spoon the dressing over the cut surfaces.

Serves 4–8

butternut squash wedges

1 large butternut squash weighing about 1.5kg, cut in 8 wedges, seeds discarded

For the marinade:

2 shallots, finely chopped

4 garlic cloves, crushed to a paste with a little salt

1 tablespoon very finely chopped lemongrass, tender inner part of the stalk only

2 fresh kaffir leaves

finely grated zest and juice of 1 orange

finely grated zest and juice of 1 lemon

1 tablespoon fennel seeds, lightly toasted and crushed

7 tablespoons extra virgin olive oil

freshly ground black pepper

There are several kinds of squash available at different times of the year – this method of cooking is fine for them all. You don't have to peel the thinner-skinned varieties. You can also cook wedges of pumpkin in a similar way.

Serves 8

Put the wedges of squash in a large saucepan and just cover with cold water. Bring to the boil then simmer for 7–10 minutes, until just tender. Drain then dry on a clean tea towel.

Combine all the ingredients for the marinade together in a large bowl. Turn the wedges in the marinade then cover and leave in the fridge for up to 24 hours.

Shake off the excess marinade and set the wedges of squash on the barbecue grill and cook over medium-hot coals for 5–8 minutes on each side until tender and lightly charred. Brush with marinade during cooking, then spoon the rest over before serving.

grilled pak choi

4 large heads pak choi, halved lengthways

1 tablespoon vegetable oil

salt and pepper

For the dressing:

2 tablespoons clear honey

2 tablespoons light soy sauce

1 tablespoon wholegrain mustard

1 tablespoon lemon juice

1 red chilli, deseeded and finely diced

A perfect accompaniment to the oriental-influenced skewers (for example, the pork and pineapple skewers on page 87), these fragrant green leaves will provide both nutrition and colour to any barbecue.

Serves 4–8

Blanch the halved pak choi for 2 minutes, drain thoroughly and pat dry with a clean tea towel. Brush with oil and lightly season with salt and pepper.

Whisk the remaining ingredients together to make a dressing. Cover and keep both the dressing and the blanched pak choi in the fridge for up to 24 hours.

When ready to cook the pak choi, fold the green leafy ends over the stalk ends. Cook over medium-hot coals for about 2 minutes on each side until lightly charred. Serve with the dressing to spoon over.

crispy potato skins

6 medium-sized potatoes, scrubbed

3–4 tablespoons extra virgin olive oil

1 tablespoon chopped rosemary

salt and freshly ground black pepper

An alternative to jacket potatoes, this is great for a gas range barbecue and will be welcomed by all your guests, especially children. Make sure you have lots of dips and sauces ready (see pages 132–141 for ideas).

Prick the potatoes all over and rub with a little oil, then wrap each in a double thickness of kitchen foil. Cook on the barbecue with the lid down for 50–60 minutes, or in the embers until slightly softened when squeezed, then leave to cool.

(Alternatively, preheat the oven to 200°C/400°F/gas mark 6, place the pricked and oiled potatoes on a rack in the centre of the oven and bake for a similar time.)

Cut the potatoes in quarters and scoop out some of the flesh, leaving a layer of potato at least 5mm thick on the skin. Keep the potato flesh for another use.

Brush the skins all over with oil and arrange in a single layer, cut-side down on the barbecue. Cook for 5–8 minutes until crisp and golden, then turn them over and cook on the other side for a further 5–8 minutes until crispy. Season generously and sprinkle with the rosemary.

garlicky grilled courgettes

6 large courgettes, sliced lengthways into 4

4 garlic cloves, crushed to a paste with a little salt

100ml extra virgin olive oil

a handful of basil leaves, roughly chopped

½ teaspoon crushed dried chillies

salt and freshly ground black pepper

Serves 4

Courgettes are really good on a barbecue as they don't dry out when subjected to the intense heat. Serve as a side dish or starter.

Place the courgette slices in a shallow dish.

Put the garlic in a small bowl and combine with the oil, basil, crushed chillies, salt and pepper to taste. Pour over the courgettes and leave to marinate for at least 30 minutes or refrigerate for up to 24 hours.

Set the courgette slices on the barbecue and chargrill over hot coals until just tender – about 3 minutes each side, basting from time to time. Serve warm or cold.

new potatoes with lemon dressing

1kg evenly sized new potatoes, scrubbed

For the dressing:

100ml olive oil

finely grated zest 1 lemon

2 tablespoons lemon juice

2 garlic cloves, crushed with a little salt

2 tablespoons snipped chives

salt and freshly ground black pepper

Serves 6

If you've baked one too many jacket potatoes, here's a great recipe for grilling new potatoes on skewers. Potatoes, chives and lemon are a classic combination and this is a really fresh, tangy recipe.

Steam or cook the potatoes in boiling salted water for about 20 minutes until just tender – they must be fully cooked. Drain thoroughly

While the potatoes are cooking, whisk together all the ingredients for the dressing except the chives. Toss the potatoes in the dressing and leave until required. They can be covered and refrigerated for up to 24 hours.

When ready to cook, thread the potatoes onto 6 long metal skewers, reserving the dressing, and cook over medium-hot coals for 2–3 minutes on each side until lightly charred,

Mix the chives into the reserved dressing and add extra lemon juice and seasoning to taste, if wished. Spoon over the potatoes and serve at once.

I particularly like these served with tomato and chilli butter, but there are plenty of other butters to choose from (see page 41). Small potatoes (about 125g) will take no more than 30 minutes. Large ones will take up to 1 hour. Timings will always vary depending on the size of the potatoes, the heat of the embers and the position of the potatoes in those embers.

Put all the ingredients for the tomato and chilli butter except the butter in a food-processor, season with about ½ teaspoon salt, and whizz until combined. Add the butter and pulse until combined. Transfer to a piece of kitchen foil or clingfilm and shape into a log about 3cm in diameter. Wrap and chill until required, or freeze for up to 1 month.

Scrub the sweet potatoes, prick all over with a fork and wrap each in a double thickness of lightly oiled kitchen foil. Place in the embers of the barbecue and cook for 30–45 minutes, turning regularly, until tender when tested with a skewer.

Carefully peel away the foil, cut a line in the top of each potato and push on the sides to open them up slightly and reveal the orange flesh. Top each one with a generous slice of tomato and chilli butter.

Serves 8

baked sweet potatoes

8 small – medium-sized sweet potatoes (red skin, orange flesh)

For the tomato and chilli butter:

2 tablespoons chopped flat-leaf parsley

2 garlic cloves, roughly chopped

4 sun-dried tomatoes, drained

2 red chillies, deseeded and roughly chopped

2 teaspoons rosemary leaves

1 tablespoon lemon juice

½ teaspoon chilli powder

250g unsalted butter, diced, then allowed to come to room temperature

½ teaspoon salt

Another great side dish, easy to make and with lots of flavour, so they won't be overlooked. Large spring onions (sometimes called salad onions) can also be cooked in this way.

Blanch the leeks for 3 minutes in boiling salted water, drain and lightly squeeze dry on a clean tea towel.

Brush the leeks with oil and chargrill on the barbecue for about 5 minutes, turning occasionally, until tender and golden on all sides.

Place the leeks in a shallow dish, and toss with the chopped parsley, the remaining oil and a splash of vinegar. Season generously with pepper then scatter with the chopped hard-boiled egg and black olives.

16 small baby leeks, trimmed

4 tablespoons olive oil

4 tablespoons roughly chopped flat-leaf parsley

a splash of sherry vinegar

3 eggs, hard-boiled and roughly chopped

a handful of black olives, stoned

freshly ground black pepper

The sauce will take more time than barbecuing the asparagus, but it is well worth it for a sophisticated lunch dish. Blanching asparagus helps to 'set' its fresh green colour.

Lay the asparagus spears in a large frying pan and cover with boiling salted water. Bring back to the boil then drain and refresh in iced water. Drain and dry on a clean tea towel. You will need to do this in batches.

For the maltaise sauce, put the orange juice in a small saucepan and boil until reduced to about two tablespoons. Transfer to a small dish and cover.

In another small saucepan boil the vinegar, 1 tablespoon of cold water and a generous pinch of ground white pepper until reduced to about 1 teaspoon. Add 2 tablespoons of cold water and the reserved orange juice and leave to cool slightly.

Whisk the egg yolks into the orange vinegar liquid, then pour this into a liquidiser goblet. Melt the butter in the saucepan used for the vinegar until it is completely melted and bubbling, then with the liquidiser running, slowly pour in the butter and continue processing until you have a thick and creamy sauce. Stir in the orange liqueur and season to taste. If the sauce is too thick you can thin it with a little boiling water.

Brush the asparagus spears with oil and season lightly. Chargrill on the barbecue for 3–5 minutes, turning occasionally. Serve at once with the maltaise sauce.

32–40 large asparagus spears, woody ends removed

vegetable oil, for brushing

salt and freshly ground black pepper

For the maltaise sauce:

juice of 2 oranges

1 tablespoon white wine vinegar

3 egg yolks

250g unsalted butter, diced

1 teaspoon orange liqueur (Orange Curaçao or Grand Marnier)

ground white pepper

chargrilled mixed vegetables

1 large aubergine, sliced lengthways

2 large courgettes, sliced lengthways

8 spring onions, blanched for 2 minutes in boiling salted water

1 red pepper, deseeded and cut into 4

1 yellow pepper, deseeded and cut into 4

12 asparagus spears, trimmed and peeled if preferred

extra virgin olive oil, for brushing

salt and freshly ground black pepper

For the dressing:

1 shallot, peeled and finely chopped

1 red chilli, deseeded and finely chopped

3 garlic cloves, finely chopped

8 basil leaves, ripped

8 tablespoons extra virgin olive oil

2 tablespoons sherry vinegar

This is a simpler marinade than the one on page 99, but this recipe will make a quick batch of chargrilled vegetables to accompany your burgers and skewers and will taste good even when cold.

Brush the vegetables with oil, season with salt and pepper and cook on the barbecue grill on both sides until lightly charred and tender. Timings will vary according to the vegetable, about 3–5 minutes.

Combine all the ingredients for the dressing in a bowl and season to taste.

Spoon the dressing over the vegetables and serve at room temperature.

salad bar

chickpea and avocado salad

2 hard-boiled egg yolks,
pushed through a sieve

6 tablespoons extra virgin
olive oil

2 tablespoons red wine
vinegar

1 small red onion, finely
chopped

1 garlic clove, crushed to a
paste with a little salt

4 tablespoons chopped
flat-leaf parsley

1 tablespoon small capers,
rinsed and drained

1 x 400g tin chickpeas,
drained and rinsed

1 ripe avocado, peeled,
stoned and cut into chunky
dice

salt and freshly ground
black pepper

Avocado goes brown quickly once it's cut and exposed to air, so have all
the other ingredients ready in advance, then put this salad together at the
last minute.

Place the sieved yolks in a large bowl and beat in the oil and vinegar. Gently fold in the
remaining ingredients and serve at once.

french bean salad

300g french beans

½ small red onion, or 1–2
shallots, halved and sliced

For the dressing:

1 tablespoon mirin

1 tablespoon soy sauce

2 tablespoons toasted
sesame oil

2 teaspoons finely chopped
fresh ginger

1 garlic clove, finely chopped

1 red chilli, deseeded and
finely chopped

2 tablespoons sesame seeds,
toasted in a dry frying pan

A lovely summer recipe, the onions and dressing will give the beans
a satisfying bite.

Whisk together all the dressing ingredients.

Trim the tops of the beans, then steam or cook in boiling salted water for about 5 minutes
until just tender. Drain thoroughly and halve the beans if wished, then mix with the onion
and the dressing. Serve warm or cold.

raw courgette and parmesan salad

It's easy to forget that courgettes are great raw. They're delicious served in a dressing such as this one, similar to the classic Caesar dressing. Serve with little gem lettuce hearts.

Serves 4

Put the grated courgette in a bowl.

To make the dressing, put the egg yolks in a liquidiser goblet, and blend with the anchovies, garlic, mustard and lemon juice. With the motor running, add the olive oil in a thin stream. Season to taste with black pepper. If the dressing is too thick, thin it with a little boiled water.

Toss the courgettes with enough dressing to coat them liberally, then fold in the grated parmesan and scatter plenty of ripped basil over the top of the salad.

350g courgettes, grated

50g fresh parmesan cheese, grated

ripped basil leaves, to garnish

For the dressing:

2 raw egg yolks

25g tinned anchovy fillets, drained and finely chopped

1 garlic clove, finely chopped

1 teaspoon English mustard

juice of ½ lemon

120ml extra virgin olive oil

freshly ground black pepper

a variation on coleslaw

I've used apple instead of carrot here, but you will still get the same sweetness as well as a beautiful rich colour to contrast with the Savoy cabbage. Delicious.

Serves 6

Place the shredded cabbage in a large bowl. Whisk the vinegar and sugar together to dissolve the sugar, then toss with the cabbage. Set aside for 1 hour.

Fold the apple into the sugar and cabbage mixture, then add enough of the mayonnaise dressing to coat and mix well. Season to taste, cover and chill for 1 hour. Mix again just before serving.

½ large Savoy cabbage or white cabbage, very finely shredded

2 tablespoons cider or white wine vinegar

2 teaspoons golden caster sugar

2 dessert apples, such as Cox, cored and diced

mayonnaise dressing, see page 141

salt and freshly ground black pepper

Fresh beansprouts are always improved by soaking in ice-cold water for 5–10 minutes – it makes them more crunchy. Mix the salad with the dressing no more than 30 minutes before serving.

To make the vinaigrette, place the lemongrass, vinegar and sugar in a small saucepan and bring to the boil. Simmer over medium heat until the liquid is reduced by about half – about 10 minutes. Remove from the heat and strain, discarding the lemongrass. Add the remaining vinaigrette ingredients, mix well and chill until ready to use.

Combine all the slaw ingredients in a large bowl and toss thoroughly. Add the vinaigrette and mix well.

vietnamese green mango slaw

2 large green (unripe, hard) mangoes, peeled, stoned and cut into matchsticks

1 large carrot, peeled and cut into matchsticks

175g bean sprouts

1 small red onion, halved then thinly sliced

2 tablespoons roughly chopped mint

2 tablespoons roughly chopped coriander leaves

1 tablespoon roughly torn basil

For the vinaigrette:

4 stalks lemongrass, finely chopped

4 tablespoons rice wine vinegar

2 tablespoons golden caster sugar

finely grated zest and juice of 2 limes

2 tablespoons finely chopped fresh green chilli

½ teaspoon finely chopped garlic

4 tablespoons fish sauce (nam pla)

salad of asparagus, avocado and pecans

24 asparagus spears, trimmed

2 avocados, halved, stoned and peeled

2 heads of chicory

100g lamb's lettuce, watercress or rocket

6 tablespoons roughly broken pecans

3 tablespoons snipped chives

For the dressing:

4 tablespoons fresh lemon juice

4 tablespoons light soy sauce

½ tablespoon grated fresh ginger

1 garlic clove, crushed with a little salt

100ml extra virgin olive oil

salt and freshly ground black pepper

This is a posh salad that looks far more difficult to make than it actually is and will go well with chicken and salmon dishes or as a starter or light lunch. The chicory and pecan nuts will give the salad texture.

Cook the asparagus in boiling water for about 6 minutes, until just tender. Drain and refresh in iced water. Drain and dry on a clean tea towel.

For the dressing, whizz 2 tablespoons of the lemon juice, the soy sauce, ginger, garlic and oil in a liquidiser goblet for 30 seconds. If too thick, add 1–2 tablespoons boiling water. Season to taste.

Slice the avocado and carefully toss with the remaining lemon juice.

Tear the chicory leaves and mix with the lamb's lettuce. Toss with some of the dressing, then arrange on a serving dish. Top with the asparagus and avocado, then sprinkle with the pecans and chives. Drizzle with a little more dressing, if you wish. Serve at once.

warm broccoli salad

1 small onion, grated

4 anchovy fillets, mashed

2 teaspoons capers, rinsed and chopped

juice of ½ lemon

3 tablespoons extra virgin olive oil

1 teaspoon chopped mint

300g broccoli, broken into small florets

freshly ground black pepper

Serving a salad warm really enhances the flavour of the ingredients. The dressing will brighten up the broccoli to make an ideal accompaniment to most barbecued meat or fish.

In a bowl, combine the onion, anchovies, capers, lemon juice, olive oil and mint.

Steam or cook the broccoli in plenty of boiling salted water for 2–3 minutes until only just tender. Drain thoroughly, then season with pepper and toss with the prepared ingredients. Serve at once.

warm rice salad

A rice salad is a great way to add some carby bulk to the traditional barbecued burgers and sausages. Serve as a side dish or starter.

Serves 6

Whisk together the dressing ingredients.

Cook the rice according to packet instructions, then while still warm, mix with all the remaining ingredients and toss with the dressing. Season to taste and serve at once.

200g basmati rice, brown or white

3 spring onions, thinly sliced

a small handful of mint leaves, chopped

a small handful of flat-leaf parsley, chopped

1 red pepper, deseeded and diced

1 yellow pepper, deseeded and diced

3 plum tomatoes, deseeded and diced

For the dressing:

1 tablespoon lemon juice or white wine vinegar

4 tablespoons light olive oil

salt and freshly ground black pepper

cabbage and jicama salad

Jicama is popular in Chinese and South American recipes and is usually served raw. It has a thin brown skin and a crisp, sweet and juicy white flesh. The texture is reminiscent of asian pears, which make a good alternative if you can't find jicama.

Serves 6

Whisk together the vinaigrette ingredients. Toss the shredded cabbage and jicama with the dressing and sprinkle with the snipped chives.

¼ head white cabbage, shredded

1 medium jicama (275–325g), peeled and cut into matchsticks

2 tablespoons snipped chives

For the vinaigrette:

juice of 2 limes

1 tablespoon finely chopped shallots

6 tablespoons extra virgin olive oil

salt and freshly ground black pepper

savoy salad

500g Savoy cabbage, finely shredded

1 small red onion, diced

250g new potatoes, cooked and sliced

For the dressing:

2 garlic cloves, crushed to a paste with a little salt

2 teaspoons chopped ginger

juice of 2 lemons

5 tablespoons extra virgin olive oil

1 tablespoon fennel seeds

1 tablespoons chopped dill

salt and freshly ground black pepper

Another good salad to balance the overwhelming meatiness of most barbecues. The savoy cabbage and red onion will complement strongly flavoured meats.

Combine the cabbage, onion and potatoes in a large bowl.

Whisk the dressing ingredients together and toss through the salad. Season to taste with salt and freshly ground black pepper.

Serves 6

chinese cabbage salad

1 head of Chinese cabbage, torn in bite-size pieces

4 spring onions, sliced

grated zest of 1 orange

2 tablespoons sesame seeds

2 tablespoons chopped mint

2 tablespoons roughly chopped coriander leaves

For the dressing:

juice of 1 orange

2 tablespoons vegetable oil

1 tablespoon sesame oil

1 tablespoon soy sauce

1 tablespoon rice wine vinegar

1 teaspoon grated ginger

1 red chilli, deseeded and chopped

Orange zest gives this salad a refreshing taste and boiling the juice intensifies the flavour of the dressing – it's good with pork and sausages.

Toast the sesame seeds in a dry frying pan.

To make the dressing, boil the orange juice in a small saucepan until reduced to about 1 tablespoon. Remove from the heat and whisk in the remaining dressing ingredients.

Combine all the salad ingredients in a large bowl and toss with the dressing. Season to taste with salt and freshly ground black pepper.

Serves 4–6

thai cucumber salad

Perfect with fish and oriental-style skewers and kebabs, this is a great-looking salad with a fantastic fresh taste.

Serves 6

Cut the cucumber into 5mm slices.

In a bowl, dissolve the sugar in the vinegar and toss the cucumber in this mixture. Fold in the chillies, shallots and coriander leaves.

Sprinkle with the peanuts and add the fish sauce just before serving.

2 cucumbers, peeled, sliced lengthways and deseeded

40g golden caster sugar

3 tablespoons rice wine vinegar

2 hot red chillies, deseeded and finely diced

2 shallots, finely diced

2 tablespoons coriander leaves

40g roasted peanuts, chopped

½ tablespoon fish sauce (nam pla)

crunchy thai salad

This is a sturdier salad than the one above and will go well with meaty burgers and skewers. Remove the seeds from the chillies if you want a milder kick.

Serves 4–6

Heat a dry frying pan, add the rice and the dried chillies and toast until the rice is golden but not burnt. Grind in a clean coffee-grinder or pound to a powder with a mortar and pestle, and set aside.

In a small bowl, dissolve the sugar in the lime juice and fish sauce. In a large bowl, combine the cucumber, shallots, cherry tomatoes, fresh chillies, herbs and spring onions. Add the lime juice mixture to taste and toss to combine.

Add the ground rice mixture and toss through the salad.

1 tablespoon uncooked jasmine rice

2 dried red chillies

2 teaspoons golden caster sugar

4 tablespoons lime juice

3 tablespoons Thai fish sauce (nam pla)

1 small cucumber, peeled, halved lengthways, deseeded and cut into 1cm slices

4 red shallots, peeled and thinly sliced

12 cherry tomatoes, halved

2 fresh red chillies, deseeded and thinly sliced

1 handful mint leaves, shredded

a handful of coriander leaves

2 tablespoons basil leaves, ripped

4 spring onions, sliced

chicory and orange nut salad

4 oranges

4 chicory heads, torn

125g seedless grapes

50g walnut pieces

50g slivered almonds

6 dates, stoned and
chopped

For the dressing:

3 tablespoons lime juice
or orange juice

2 tablespoons clear honey

½ teaspoon ground
cinnamon

3 tablespoons walnut oil

3 tablespoons shredded
mint leaves

salt and freshly ground
black pepper

Try toasting the nuts – it brings out their flavour and makes them more crunchy. Soaking chicory leaves in ice-cold water for 15 minutes will improve their crunchiness. Drain and dry them thoroughly before making the salad.

Using a small serrated knife, peel the oranges to remove all the white pith. Cut them in half vertically then slice thinly. Combine with the chicory, grapes, nuts and dates.

Whisk all the dressing ingredients together and just before serving, gently toss the salad. Season to taste.

This is a substantial salad that goes really well with veggie kebabs and lamb burgers.

In a medium-sized bowl, combine the beans with all the remaining ingredients and toss to mix. Season to taste.

Serves 6

cannellini bean and pecorino salad

2 x 400g tins cannellini beans, drained and rinsed

3 tablespoons extra virgin olive oil

1 tablespoon freshly squeezed lemon juice

1 teaspoon dried oregano

3 tablespoons roughly chopped flat-leaf parsley

a generous pinch of dried crushed chillies

250g pecorino or hard goat's cheese, cut into small cubes

salt and freshly ground black pepper

Jersey Royals are delicious when available – otherwise there is a great variety of salad potatoes to choose from such as Charlotte, Pink Fir and Nicola.

Steam or boil the potatoes in salted water until tender, about 15–20 minutes. Drain and keep warm.

Fry the lardons in a dry non-stick pan until crisp, then add the shallots and cook just until softened but not browned. Deglaze the pan with the red wine vinegar, then add the olive oil, pickled cucumbers and mustard.

Toss the potatoes in this dressing. Sprinkle with the parsley and season to taste.

Serves 4–6

new potato salad

750g small new potatoes, scrubbed

250g streaky bacon, derinded and cut into lardons

2 shallots, peeled and finely diced

1 tablespoon red wine vinegar

4 tablespoons extra virgin olive oil

2 sweet-pickled cucumbers, finely diced

2 teaspoons wholegrain mustard

1 tablespoon finely chopped flat-leaf parsley

salt and freshly ground black pepper

fennel and red grapefruit salad

4 ruby red grapefruit

2 fennel bulbs, trimmed and very thinly sliced

6 spring onions, thinly sliced

1 teaspoon ground cumin

4 tablespoons extra virgin olive oil

18 Kalamata olives (optional)

1 teaspoon salt

Fennel is a wonderful vegetable that is great grilled, roasted or stir-fried, but is a revelation when dressed and eaten raw. A mandolin makes it so easy to get paper-thin slices, but watch your fingers!

Over a large bowl, peel the grapefruit with a small serrated knife to remove all the white pith. Cut between the membranes to remove the segments, discarding the seeds and any more pith. (Squeeze the peelings and reserve all the juice to drink.)

Halve each grapefruit segment if preferred, then transfer to a serving bowl. Sprinkle with salt.

Combine the fennel with the grapefruit. Add the spring onions, cumin and olive oil. Garnish with the olives, if using.

carrot and celeriac salad

250g carrots, peeled and grated

250g celeriac, peeled and grated

4 tablespoons mayonnaise

4 tablespoons soured cream or natural yogurt

1 tablespoon wholegrain mustard

1 teaspoon English mustard

salt and freshly ground black pepper

Celeriac is an under-used and underrated root vegetable with a distinct celery flavour – do try it. You might also try adding some grated apple, a few raisins or toasted chopped nuts to the salad.

Combine the carrots and celeriac in a bowl.

Mix together the remaining ingredients and season generously. Toss through the carrot mixture until evenly coated.

herbed leaf salad

There's a fantastic choice of salad leaves available to give amazing flavour to a simple leaf salad, but make sure all the leaves are dry before dressing them. A salad-spinner is one of my 'can't do without' pieces of equipment, but if you haven't got one try my grandmother's trick of shaking the leaves in a clean pillowcase. Be careful with the dressing – it should merely 'kiss' the leaves to make them glisten, not drown them.

Serves 6

Tear any large leaves into bite-size pieces and, in a large bowl, combine all the salad leaves with the herbs. Season lightly.

To make the shallot vinaigrette, combine the vinegar, shallot and some salt and pepper in a bowl, then slowly whisk in the oils.

Toss the salad with sufficient dressing to make the leaves glisten. Serve at once.

300g assorted salad leaves (such as mizuna, lamb's lettuce, baby spinach, rocket, baby chard, watercress, curly endive, lettuce)

4 tablespoons fresh herbs (such as chervil, tarragon, dill, basil, mint, chives)

salt and freshly ground black pepper

For the hazelnut shallot vinaigrette:

2 tablespoons sherry vinegar

1 small shallot, finely diced

3 tablespoons hazelnut oil

3 tablespoons light olive oil

salt and freshly ground black pepper

tomato and basil salad

Ensure that the tomatoes are not chilled – their flavour is always much better at room temperature. Plum tomatoes generally have a good flavour, but try experimenting with all the different varieties available. You can also add some yellow, orange or red cherry tomatoes to this salad.

Serves 4–6

Slice the tomatoes and arrange on a serving dish. Scatter the chopped anchovies, if using, over them, along with the basil and onion.

Drizzle with the oil and vinegar and season to taste.

6 large, ripe, firm tomatoes

2 anchovy fillets, finely chopped (optional)

12 basil leaves, ripped

1 small red onion, diced

3 tablespoons extra virgin olive oil

1 teaspoon balsamic vinegar

salt and freshly ground black pepper

spicy tomato and bread salad

6 plum tomatoes, peeled, deseeded and diced

½ cucumber, peeled, deseeded and roughly diced

50g flat-leaf parsley, chopped

4 tablespoons chopped mint

2 red peppers, roasted, peeled, deseeded and roughly diced

3 medium-hot chillies, deseeded and diced

2 tablespoons salted capers, rinsed, drained and chopped

1 pitta bread, toasted and finely shredded

100g feta cheese, cubed

For the dressing:

5 tablespoons extra virgin olive oil

1 tablespoon lemon juice

1 tablespoon balsamic vinegar

2 teaspoons finely grated orange zest

2 tablespoons pink peppercorns, crushed

1 garlic clove, crushed with a little salt

2 teaspoons harissa or chilli paste

salt and freshly ground black pepper

This is my version of a classic Italian recipe. A hearty salad, this is great as part of a veggie main course or side dish for a warm summer lunch.

In a small bowl, whisk together all the dressing ingredients.

In a large bowl, combine the tomatoes, cucumber, parsley, mint, peppers, chillies and capers and toss with the dressing.

Pile the salad onto a large serving dish and top with the shredded pitta bread and the feta cheese.

Serves 6

thai-inspired waldorf salad

2 dessert apples (Cox, Braeburn, Granny Smith), cored and diced

1 cucumber, peeled (optional), deseeded and diced

6 spring onions, sliced

12 radishes, trimmed and sliced

2 tablespoons roughly chopped coriander leaves

2 tablespoon grated fresh ginger

4 tablespoon lime juice

2 teaspoons clear honey

2 garlic cloves, finely chopped

2 tablespoons extra virgin olive oil

4 teaspoons toasted sesame oil

1 teaspoon chilli oil

2 heads of chicory, ripped into small pieces

2 tablespoons roughly chopped macadamia nuts

salt

A traditional Waldorf salad would include apples, walnuts, raisins and celery, but I have created an Asian-fusion version with a bit of spice. Add more chilli oil if you like.

In a large bowl, combine all the ingredients except the chicory, nuts and salt. Season with salt then cover and chill for up to 1 hour, or until the natural juices are released.

Just before serving, stir in the chicory.

Serves 4–6

Onions are great on a barbecue as the strong heat brings out their naturally sweet flavour. Try mixing this with grilled asparagus spears. To reduce the cooking time on the barbecue, blanch the onions first.

To make the marinade, in a small bowl combine the oil, vinegar, half the lemon zest and all the juice, the cumin and the coriander. Place the onions in a shallow dish and brush the marinade mixture over them. Marinate for at least 30 minutes, or, covered, in the fridge overnight.

Place the onion halves on the barbecue and cook over a medium-low heat for about 12 minutes each side, brushing occasionally with any leftover marinade, until tender.

Cool the onions slightly then sprinkle with the remaining lemon zest, and season with salt and pepper. Serve at room temperature.

spicy barbecued onion salad

4 medium-sized red onions, peeled, then sliced in half horizontally

salt and freshly ground black pepper

For the marinade:

1 tablespoon extra virgin olive oil

1 teaspoon balsamic vinegar

grated zest of 1 lemon

juice of ½ lemon

1 teaspoon ground cumin

1 teaspoon ground coriander

sauces, salsas & dips

american barbecue sauce

4 tablespoons vegetable oil

2 onions, finely chopped

3 celery stalks, finely chopped

2 tablespoons chopped garlic

1 carrot, finely chopped

1 teaspoon thyme leaves

175ml cider vinegar

175ml tomato ketchup

6 tablespoons tomato purée

4 tablespoons soy sauce

1 tablespoon Worcestershire sauce

½ tablespoon chilli powder

4 tablespoons unrefined soft dark brown sugar

1 teaspoon ground cumin

1 teaspoon paprika

1 teaspoon salt

Heat the vegetable oil in a large saucepan. Add the onion, celery, garlic, carrot and thyme and cook for 10 minutes over a moderate heat until the vegetables have softened without colouring.

Add the remaining ingredients and simmer until the vegetables are soft, about 20 minutes. The sauce should be quite thick. Purée the sauce in a liquidiser or blender, if wished.

barbecue sauce

Great for spare ribs and chicken. It will keep in the fridge for up to 10 days or may be frozen for up to 1 month.

1 onion, chopped

4 garlic cloves, finely chopped

2 tablespoons fennel seeds

2 red chillies, deseeded and finely chopped

2 tablespoons vegetable oil

600ml tomato ketchup

150ml soy sauce

175g unrefined soft dark brown sugar

In a large saucepan, cook the onion, garlic, fennel seeds and chillies in the oil over a moderate heat until softened but not browned. Add the remaining ingredients and simmer for about 30–40 minutes, stirring occasionally. The sauce should be quite thick but add a little water now and again if it's getting too thick.

blue cheese dip

142ml carton soured cream

150ml mayonnaise

2 teaspoons white wine vinegar

2 tablespoons sliced spring onions

1 garlic clove, finely diced

1 teaspoon Tabasco sauce

75g crumbled blue cheese (Stilton, Roquefort, blue Auvergne)

salt and freshly ground pepper

In a food-processor, blend together the soured cream, mayonnaise, vinegar, spring onions, garlic, Tabasco and the cheese. Season to taste.

tomato and white wine sauce

3 tablespoons olive oil

300ml tomato passata

300ml dry white wine

salt and freshly ground black pepper

Heat the oil in a saucepan and when hot add the passata and wine and simmer, uncovered, for 15 minutes, stirring occasionally. Season to taste and serve warm.

spicy tomato sauce

This will keep for two weeks in the fridge.

3 small red chillies, deseeded if preferred to reduce the heat and roughly chopped

2 red peppers, deseeded and roughly chopped

2 garlic cloves, crushed with a little salt

½ tablespoon grated fresh ginger

1 shallot, roughly chopped

1 tablespoon fish sauce (nam pla)

1 x 400g tin chopped tomatoes with juice

100g unrefined dark soft brown sugar

3 tablespoons sherry vinegar

Put the chillies, red peppers, garlic, ginger, shallot, fish sauce and tomatoes in a food-processor and blend until smooth.

Put this purée with the sugar and vinegar in a stainless steel or other non-reactive saucepan and bring to the boil, stirring from time to time. Reduce the heat and simmer for 40–60 minutes until thick. Stir regularly, especially in the latter stages of cooking.

If you prefer a smooth consistency, strain the sauce through a fine sieve. Bottle in warm sterilised jars. Allow to cool, then refrigerate until needed.

cucumber sauce

1 large cucumber, peeled, deseeded and finely chopped

½ teaspoon salt

1 teaspoon red wine vinegar

1 teaspoon golden caster sugar

200ml soured cream

1 teaspoon Dijon mustard

1 shallot, finely chopped

1 tablespoon chopped dill

Put the cucumber in a colander. Sprinkle with the salt, vinegar and the sugar. Leave to stand for 30 minutes. Lightly rinse with cold water. Drain, pressing out excess liquid with the back of a spoon.

In a medium-sized bowl, beat the soured cream with the mustard, then stir in the shallot, dill and cucumber. Cover and chill until ready to serve.

cucumber raita

½ large cucumber, coarsely grated

200g Greek-style yogurt

2 tablespoons finely chopped dill

1 teaspoon crushed black pepper

1 small garlic clove, crushed with a pinch of salt

1 tablespoon vegetable oil

½ teaspoon mustard seeds

½ teaspoon cumin seeds

pinch of asafoetida (optional)

4–5 fresh curry leaves

Squeeze out any excess water from the grated cucumber, then mix together with the yogurt, dill, pepper and garlic.

Heat the oil in a small frying pan and fry the mustard seeds, cumin seeds, curry leaves and asafoetida just until the seeds start to pop and become fragrant. Stir into the raita.

vegetable raita

1 cucumber, peeled, deseeded and diced

1 plum tomato, deseeded and diced

1 small onion, very finely chopped

1 cooked potato, peeled and diced

½ teaspoon cumin seeds, dry-roasted

425ml Greek-style yogurt

1 tablespoon chopped mint

salt and freshly ground black pepper

Combine all the ingredients. Season to taste, cover and and chill until required. To store, cover and refrigerate for up to 2 days.

sweet and sour dipping sauce

A make-ahead sauce that will reheat well – set aside the spring onions and add them when you warm the sauce.

4 tablespoons golden caster sugar

3 tablespoons rice wine vinegar

2 tablespoons tomato ketchup

2 teaspoons soy sauce

2 tablespoons vegetable oil

1 tablespoon finely chopped garlic

2 teaspoons finely chopped fresh ginger

2 teaspoons cornflour mixed with
  2 tablespoons cold water

3 spring onions, thinly sliced

salt and freshly ground black pepper

Place the sugar in a bowl, pour in 150ml boiling water and stir to dissolve, then stir in the vinegar, ketchup and soy sauce.

In a small saucepan, heat the oil and stir-fry the garlic and ginger for 30 seconds. Add the sweetened liquids and bring to the boil, then reduce the heat and stir in the cornflour mixture. Stir the sauce over the heat for a further 30 seconds until thickened, then fold in the spring onions and season to taste. Serve warm.

coriander dipping sauce

Best served on the day of making. Great with chicken and fish.

a handful of coriander leaves, chopped

4 spring onions, finely chopped

1 tablespoon grated fresh ginger

1 green chilli, deseeded and finely chopped

1 garlic clove, crushed

4 tablespoons light soy sauce

4 tablespoons vegetable oil

freshly ground black pepper

Whisk all the ingredients together except the seasoning then thin, if wished with boiled water to give a dipping consistency. Season to taste.

oriental dipping sauce

Great with chicken kebabs, but make on the day.

1 teaspoon chopped coriander leaves

3 spring onions, very thinly sliced

1 teaspoon very thinly sliced shallot

1 teaspoon grated fresh ginger

1 garlic clove, finely chopped

1 green chilli, deseeded and finely diced

2 tablespoons lime juice

2 tablespoons light soy sauce

1 teaspoon sesame oil

1 tablespoon clear honey

Mix all the ingredients together. Cover and set aside until ready to serve.

oriental mustard sauce

Great with steaks and sausages or root vegetable kebabs.

5 tablespoons wholegrain mustard

5 tablespoons Dijon mustard

150ml toasted sesame oil

1 tablespoon mirin or dry sherry

2 tablespoons finely chopped spring onion

3 tablespoons chopped coriander leaves

salt and freshly ground black pepper

Whisk the mustards, sesame oil and mirin together until smooth (or whizz in a blender goblet). Stir in the remaining ingredients and season to taste. Store in the fridge for up to 48 hours.

chilli peanut sauce

175g smooth peanut butter

4 tablespoons sweet soy sauce (katchup manis)

2 tablespoons clear honey

1 teaspoon chilli oil

4 tablespoons rice vinegar

Blend all the ingredients together until smooth. Thin down to a sauce consistency with boiled water. Cover and chill until required.

coriander mint chutney

This is best eaten fresh. It's also great mixed with a few generous dollops of thick Greek yogurt to make a dip. Serve it with warmed pitta bread or other flat breads.

50g mint leaves

75g coriander leaves

1 small onion, chopped

3cm piece of fresh ginger, peeled and chopped

1 green chilli, deseeded and chopped

½ teaspoon cumin seeds

1 garlic clove, chopped

1 teaspoon salt

2 teaspoons lemon juice

1 tablespoon desiccated coconut

Blend all the ingredients together in a food-processor until fairly smooth, then store in an airtight container in the fridge until needed.

aubergine, red pepper & herb salsa

1 large aubergine

6 tablespoons vegetable oil

6 tablespoons soy sauce

6 tablespoons rice vinegar

2 red peppers, roasted, peeled, deseeded and diced

2 tablespoons fish sauce (nam pla)

2 tablespoons unrefined soft dark brown sugar

1 teaspoon Chinese chilli sauce

6 spring onions, very thinly sliced

1 tablespoon grated fresh ginger

2 tablespoons chopped coriander leaves

1 tablespoon chopped mint

2 tablespoons chopped flat-leaf parsley

3 garlic cloves, finely chopped

1 teaspoon finely grated lemon zest

Cut the aubergine into 5mm slices and combine with the vegetable oil, soy sauce and vinegar. Leave to marinate for 1 hour, turning and basting regularly. Drain thoroughly, reserving the marinade.

Cook the aubergine slices over a barbecue, or alternatively on a griddle pan or frying pan over a medium-high heat for 2–3 minutes on each side. They should be very dark and thoroughly cooked. Allow to cool.

Dice the aubergine slices to match the red pepper dice. Combine the peppers and aubergine together with the reserved marinade and the remaining ingredients. Serve at room temperature on the day of making.

salsa verde

a handful of flat-leaf parsley, roughly chopped

2 tablespoons roughly chopped fresh mint

2 shallots, peeled and finely chopped

1 tablespoon finely chopped fresh rosemary

1 tablespoon capers, rinsed and chopped

½ teaspoon anchovy paste

½ teaspoon crushed dried chilli

2 tablespoons red wine vinegar

175ml extra virgin olive oil

salt and freshly ground black pepper

Combine all the salsa verde ingredients except the oil and salt and pepper in a food-processor. With the motor running, drizzle in the oil to make a thin sauce. Add salt and pepper to taste and whizz again briefly. Cover and chill until required. Best served fresh.

mango salsa

Salsas are made up of fresh, mainly raw ingredients which release their juices when chopped. It is therefore best to serve them on the day of making.

1 large ripe mango, peeled, stoned, diced
a small handful of mint leaves, chopped
a small handful of coriander leaves, chopped
juice of 1 lime
1 small red onion, peeled and diced
1 red chilli, deseeded and chopped
2 tomatoes, deseeded and diced
dash of extra virgin olive oil
salt and freshly ground black pepper

Combine all the ingredients. Serve at room temperature.

fennel salsa

This is great served freshly made with grilled fish. Remove the tough outer layer of the fennel with a vegetable peeler before dicing.

1 fennel bulb, finely diced
2 tomatoes, deseeded and diced
2 teaspoons capers, rinsed, drained and chopped
2 teaspoons chopped black olives
3 spring onions, thinly sliced
2 tablespoons chopped flat-leaf parsley
1 tablespoon snipped fennel or dill herb
4 tablespoons extra virgin olive oil
salt and freshly ground black pepper

Combine all the ingredients and season to taste. Serve at room temperature.

red salsa

If the salsa is too thick for your taste, add a little tomato juice to thin it to the required consistency.

8 plum tomatoes, deseeded and diced
3 roasted red peppers, peeled, deseeded and diced
1 red chilli, deseeded and diced
a small handful of coriander leaves
½ red onion, diced
4 tablespoons extra virgin olive oil
juice of 1 lemon
salt and freshly ground black pepper

Combine all the ingredients in a food-processor and pulse to combine but retain the chunkiness. Season well.

tomato & avocado salsa

4 large ripe tomatoes, deseeded and finely diced
1 red chilli, deseeded and finely diced
½ teaspoon ground cumin
½ teaspoon ground coriander
juice of 1 lime
1 small red onion, finely chopped
2 medium-ripe avocados, halved, stoned, peeled and finely diced
2 tablespoons extra virgin olive oil
8 tablespoons roughly chopped coriander leaves
salt and freshly ground black pepper

Combine all the ingredients and season to taste. Best served freshly made.

horseradish cream

This will keep in the fridge for 2–3 days. Great with steaks and salmon.

142ml carton double cream
150ml mayonnaise
50–75g freshly grated horseradish (or from a jar)
2 tablespoons Dijon mustard
1 tablespoon lemon juice
pinch of unrefined sugar
salt and freshly ground black pepper

Lightly whip the cream and fold in the remaining ingredients. Season to taste. Cover and chill until required. Stir before serving.

tomato horseradish dip

150ml sweet chilli sauce
150ml tomato ketchup
1 tablespoon lemon juice
2 tablespoons grated horseradish (not creamed)
1 teaspoon Worcestershire sauce
1 celery stalk, very finely diced
dash of Tabasco sauce

Combine all the ingredients, cover and chill until ready to serve.

zhug

This hot and spicy Yemenite condiment is used for sprinkling on grilled meat. It's also great mixed into Greek yogurt to make a dip. Add more lime juice to thin as required and even a dash of boiled water when ready to use. It can be stored in a jar in the fridge for up to two days.

14 green chillies, deseeded if wished to reduce the heat and chopped
12 garlic cloves
1 teaspoon caraway seeds, ground
1 teaspoon cumin seeds, ground
½ teaspoon ground cardamom
5 tablespoons chopped coriander leaves
1 tablespoon lime juice
1 teaspoon each salt and freshly ground black pepper

Place all the ingredients in a small food-processor and pulse until fairly smooth.

skordalia

Delicious with grilled aubergines and courgettes or lamb.

2 medium potatoes, weighing about 150g each, scrubbed but unpeeled
3 garlic cloves, roughly chopped
1 tablespoon lemon juice
175ml extra virgin olive oil
125ml milk
salt

Steam or cook the potatoes in boiling water until tender – 30–40 minutes. Drain and when cool enough to handle, peel and chop roughly.

Put the potatoes, garlic, the lemon juice and a generous pinch of salt in a food-processor and whizz until lightly mixed. With the motor running, add the olive oil in a thin stream until all the oil is incorporated. Add the milk slowly until combined and smooth. Serve at room temperature.

Hungarian relish

A great relish from Eastern Europe called ajuar, this is particularly good with burgers and sausages. It will keep for one month in the fridge.

2 red peppers
1 aubergine
100ml extra virgin olive oil
3 hot chillies, deseeded if wished to reduce the heat, finely chopped
3 garlic cloves, crushed with a little salt to a fine paste
4 tablespoons sherry vinegar
3 tablesoons clear honey
¼ teaspoon cayenne pepper
½ teaspoon ground cumin
½ teaspoon ground coriander
1 tablespoon chopped coriander leaves

Preheat the oven to 190°C/375°F/gas mark 5. Rub the red peppers and aubergine with 2 teaspoons of the oil. Place on a baking tray in the oven for 30–40 minutes until the red peppers are lightly charred and the aubergine is very soft. Remove from the oven, transfer to a bowl and cover with clingfilm for 10–20 minutes. When cool enough to handle, peel away the skins of both vegetables with your fingers and discard. Dice the flesh and set aside.

In a frying pan, heat the remaining olive oil over a medium heat. Add the chillies, garlic, sherry vinegar, honey, cayenne pepper, cumin and ground coriander. Mix well, then stir in the reserved peppers and aubergine with the fresh coriander. Reduce the heat and cook gently, uncovered, for about 10 minutes, stirring regularly, until very thick. Leave to cool then refrigerate until required.

pineapple sambal

Sambal is a fresh pickle which doesn't keep, so it's best eaten the day it's made.

1 pineapple, peeled and cut into
    2cm slices
1 red pepper, roasted, peeled,
    deseeded and diced
2 tablespoons sambal oelek
2 teaspoons chopped mint
2 tablespoons lime juice
1 teaspoon clear honey

1 tablespoon chopped coriander leaves
freshly ground black pepper

Chargrill the pineapple slices on the barbecue, or on a griddle pan over high heat, turning the slices occasionally while cooking. Sprinkle the slices with black pepper.

    Dice the pineapple and transfer to a bowl. Stir in the roasted pepper then add the sambal oelek, mint, lime juice and honey. Stir to combine. Finally stir in the coriander. Serve at room temperature.

avocado mayonnaise

Delicious as a dip or served with jacket potatoes, chicken or steaks.

2 ripe avocados, halved, stoned and
    peeled
juice of half a lemon
1 teaspoon grated horseradish
dash of Tabasco sauce
2 spring onions, finely chopped
1 tablespoon snipped chives
150ml mayonnaise
x1 142ml carton soured cream
salt and freshly ground black pepper

Mash the avocado with the lemon juice, then mix in the remaining ingredients and season to taste. Cover and chill until required for up to 2 days.

chilli mayonnaise

This is great with squid.

2 green or red chillies, deseeded amd
    chopped
2 garlic cloves, peeled
1 egg yolk
1 tablespoon lime juice
175ml groundnut oil
salt and freshly ground black pepper

In a small liquidiser goblet, whizz together the chillies and the garlic until smooth. Whisk in the egg yolk and lime juice, then with the motor running add the groundnut oil a few drips at a time until the mayonnaise emulsifies and becomes thick. Season to taste. Best served freshly made.

mayonnaise dressing

1 garlic clove, crushed with a little salt
2 anchovy fillets, mashed to a paste
125ml good-quality mayonnaise
125ml Greek-style yogurt
2 teaspoons Dijon mustard
1 tablespoon chopped dill

Whisk together the dressing ingredients and leave for at least 1½ hours to allow the flavours to develop.

afters & alcohol

grilled maple macadamia pears

4 medium-ripe Anjou or
Williams pears

½ lemon

chocolate or vanilla ice
cream, to serve

For the macadamia filling:

100g macadamia nuts

2 tablespoons nut brittle

2 tablespoons maple syrup,
plus extra for drizzling

1 tablespoon desiccated
coconut

2 tablespoons ricotta
cheese

½ teaspoon natural vanilla
extract

Grilled pears with a surprise in the centre – but do check if any of your guests are allergic to nuts. The crunchy filling will complement the sweet softness of the pears.

Make the macadamia filling: first, reserve 4 large whole macadamia nuts. Put the remaining nuts in a food-processor with the remaining ingredients and blend to a chunky paste. Set aside.

Peel the whole pears, and rub them well with the cut side of a lemon to prevent discolouring. With a melon baller or a small peeling knife, and working from the bottom of each pear upwards, scoop out the core leaving a cavity for the macadamia filling; do not scoop out all the way through the top. Spoon the filling into the pears then push a whole macadamia nut into the bottom of each pear to keep the filling in place.

Oil the barbecue grill and grill the pears on their sides, about 12.5cm above cool–medium hot coals in a covered barbecue, for about 8 minutes or until cooked through. Turn them over every 2–3 minutes, and baste with maple syrup from time to time.

To serve, stand the pears upright on dessert plates and serve with chocolate or vanilla ice cream.

amaretti peaches

12 amaretti biscuits or
36 ratafia biscuits

2 tablespoons Amaretto
liqueur

50g unsalted butter, cut in
small dice

4 large ripe peaches

mascarpone cheese, to
serve (optional)

White peaches have a wonderfully delicate flavour and are great cooked like this. Always start with ripe peaches – hard ones just won't cook in the same way. If you want to make the mascarpone extra special, add a dash of grappa and some icing sugar to sweeten.

Roughly crush the amaretti biscuits and mix well with the liqueur and butter.

Split the peaches in half and discard the stones. Cut 4 large squares of kitchen foil, then place 2 peach halves on each one. Spoon a little of the biscuit mixture over each peach half, then carefully wrap them up to seal in the juices.

Set on the barbecue grill over medium-hot coals and cook ideally with the lid down for 7–8 minutes until softened and heated through. Serve with mascarpone cheese, if wished.

grilled fruit kebabs

Aahh, another classic kebab and a really simple dessert recipe. Vary the fruits to suit your taste, but make sure you have a good combination of colours and shape.

In a small bowl, combine all the sugar mixture ingredients and mix until the sugar is dissolved.

Thread a single piece of each fruit onto 16 small metal skewers, or soaked wooden ones. Brush the fruit kebabs with the sugar mixture.

Grill the kebabs over medium-hot coals for 6–8 minutes, turning and basting frequently, until the fruit starts to brown and is heated through. Serve with crème fraiche or Greek-style natural yogurt.

Makes 16 small kebabs

2 green dessert apples (Granny Smith's), cored and each cut into 8 pieces

2 large bananas, peeled and each cut into 8 pieces

2 peaches or nectarines, stoned and each cut into 8 pieces

4 kiwi fruit, peeled and each cut into 4 pieces

16 large chunks of fresh pineapple

16 strawberries, washed and hulled

For the sugar mixture:

2 tablespoons vegetable oil

2 tablespoons unrefined soft brown sugar

4 tablespoons lime juice

1 teaspoon ground cinnamon

4 tablespoons finely shredded mint leaves

knickerbocker glory

I coudn't resist including this recipe – retro food is popular right now and this is so reminiscent of the 50s and 60s. Especially good for children's parties, these are sure to make your guests smile!

Divide half the mixed fruit between 4 tall glasses and top each with a scoop of vanilla ice cream. Repeat the layer again.

Spoon, or pipe, the whipped cream on top, sprinkle with nuts and stick 2 wafer rolls in the top of each glass. Serve immediately.

Makes 4

500g assorted prepared fresh fruit, diced (or use 2 x 411g cans fruit cocktail in fruit juice, drained)

8 large scoops of vanilla ice cream

1 x 284ml carton double cream or whipping cream, lightly whipped

2 tablespoons shelled pistachio nuts, roughly chopped

8 ice cream wafer rolls

4 large, ripe, firm mangoes, peeled if preferred, and flesh cut off either side of the stone

For the sorbet:

3 limes

250g golden caster sugar, plus extra for sprinkling

10 good-quality tea bags (Keemun or Orange Pekoe Ceylon work particularly well)

grilled mango with tea lime sorbet

Juicy limes are very important for this dessert. Thin-skinned limes yield the most juice, as do slightly older ones, identified by their muddy yellow colour, so it's often worth popping down to the market and seeking out older stock – at a knock-down price of course! The sorbet will keep in the freezer for up to 6 months.

To make the sorbet, pare the zest from the limes and set the limes aside. Chop the zest into tiny pieces. Place in a small pan and cover with water. Bring to the boil to blanch, then tip into a fine sieve and refresh under cold running water.

Place the sugar in a large saucepan with 1 litre water and heat over a low heat until dissolved, then boil fast to a syrup for 2–3 minutes. Remove from the heat, pour into a large bowl and set aside, retaining 150ml of the syrup in the pan. Add the blanched lime zest to the pan and simmer for about 15 minutes until completely tender, stirring occasionally and being careful not to let the syrup boil away and burn. Add to the reserved sugar syrup.

Pour 300ml water in a separate pan, add the tea bags and bring to the boil, then remove from the heat and set aside for 3–5 minutes to infuse. Taste after 3 minutes: if you are happy with the flavour, remove the tea bags; if you want it a little stronger, infuse with the tea bags for a few more minutes – just don't allow the tea to infuse for too long or it will become bitter. Strain into a jug, discarding the tea bags.

Cut the limes in half. Squeeze the juice through a fine strainer into a bowl, then stir into the lime sugar syrup. Add the tea infusion and stir to combine. Taste – you may want to add extra sugar or lime juice. Leave to cool completely.

Transfer to an ice-cream/sorbet machine and churn according to the manufacturer's instructions. Alternatively, freeze in a rigid container until half-frozen then whizz in a food-processor until smooth and freeze again.

When you are ready to serve, lightly sprinkle the cut side of each mango half with sugar. Place on the barbecue grill sugar-side down and cook for 2–3 minutes. Sprinkle some more sugar over the mango halves, turn them over and cook for a further 2–3 minutes or until the mango is lightly charred and caramelised. Arrange on plates and serve hot, with scoops of the lime sorbet.

chargrilled pineapple

Surprisingly, both peppercorns and chilli peppers go well with the sweetness of ripe pineapple. Try threading the wedges of pineapple onto skewers to make large 'lollipops'.

Combine all the sauce ingredients in a small saucepan and whisk until smooth. Bring to the boil over medium-high heat and cook until thickened, about 2–3 minutes. Keep the glaze warm, or reheat when ready to use.

Peel the pineapple, removing all the 'eyes' in the flesh. Cut into 8 wedges and discard the core. Season both sides of the pineapple wedges with the Szechwan pepper. Place on the barbecue over a medium heat until well marked, about 6–8 minutes, turning once halfway through the cooking time.

Serve 1–2 pineapple wedges with some of the sauce drizzled over the top, and a scoop of vanilla ice cream.

1 large ripe pineapple

2 teaspoons dried Szechwan peppercorns, finely ground

4–8 scoops vanilla ice cream

For the sauce:

½ teaspoon ground star anise

200ml pineapple juice, or orange juice

½ teaspoon crushed dried chillies

2 tablespoons clear honey

finely grated zest and juice of 1 lime

2 teaspoons cornflour

25g unsalted butter

date and pineapple skewers

A more grown-up fruit kebab, sweet but oh so delicious. Serve these skewers with a scoop of ice cream or natural yogurt to take the edge off the richness.

To make the marinade, put the butter in a small saucepan and melt over a low heat, along with the lemon juice, cinnamon and honey, and stir to combine. Put the pineapple and dates in a bowl, pour over the marinade and toss to combine. Leave for 1 hour before cooking. Meanwhile, soak 6 long bamboo skewers in cold water for 30 minutes.

Thread 4 pineapple chunks and 3 dates alternately onto each skewer. Place on an oiled barbecue grill over cool–medium-hot coals and cook, turning occasionally, until the pineapple is golden on all sides but without burning the dates – 3–5 minutes each side. Brush with the reserved marinade during cooking.

Serve with vanilla ice cream or natural yogurt.

1 medium-sized ripe pineapple, peeled, cored and cut in 24 date-sized chunks

18 Medjool dates, stoned

vanilla ice cream or natural yogurt, to serve (optional)

For the marinade:

100g unsalted butter, melted

juice of 1 lemon

1 teaspoon ground cinnamon

4 tablespoons clear honey

barbecued bananas

4 tablespoons unsalted butter, plus extra for greasing

4 large bananas, peeled

3 tablespoons unrefined soft brown sugar

3 tablespoons lime juice

2 tablespoons light rum

1 teaspoon ground allspice

We all remember pushing chocolate buttons into ripe bananas and roasting them, wrapped in foil, on the barbecue or in the oven – this is the adult version. This dish is lovely served with ice cream.

Cut four large squares of kitchen foil and lightly spread with butter. Cut each banana in half lengthways. Put two halves on each foil square and sprinkle with the sugar, lime juice, half of the rum and all the allspice. Dot with butter and wrap well to seal in all the juices.

Set the parcels on a hot barbecue grill rack and cook for 5–8 minutes – you want the bananas to be soft yet still retain their shape. Check the bananas halfway through their cooking time by carefully opening the foil. At this point you can also baste the bananas with their cooking juices.

To serve, open the foil parcels and sprinkle with the remaining rum.

bananas with toffee sauce

8 bananas in their skins

For the toffee sauce:

100g unsalted butter

100g unrefined soft brown sugar

1 teaspoon ground cinnamon

100ml dark rum

142ml carton double cream

A simple way of barbecuing bananas is to cook them in their skins until they blacken and feel very soft. When you cut back the skin you will discover a natural banana soufflé – delicious.

To make the toffee sauce, melt the butter in a small saucepan with the sugar, cinnamon and rum. Simmer, stirring from time to time, until the sauce begins to thicken. Add the cream and whisk until the sauce emulsifies. Do not boil.

Place the bananas, unpeeled, on the barbecue over medium heat and cook until the skins have blackened all over and are just beginning to split.

Allow your guests to peel their own bananas and watch for their excited reactions. Serve the sauce separately.

the strawberry blonde

A great alternative to a classic dessert. Make the strawberry purée and keep it covered in the fridge – for up to 48 hours.

250g ripe strawberries, washed, then hulled
75g golden caster sugar
1 bottle rosé champagne or sparkling wine, chilled
6 scoops vanilla ice cream

Liquidise the strawberries and sugar with 5 tablespoons iced water. Pass through a fine sieve.

When ready to serve, pour the strawberry purée into a large jug and add the champagne. Stir well and pour into 6 glasses. Add a scoop of ice cream to each glass.

Makes 6

margarita

A classic cocktail that is always popular.

6 lime wedges
fine salt
ice cubes
375ml tequila
200ml Cointreau or Triple Sec
250ml lime juice

Rub the rim of each Martini glass with a lime wedge, then dip in salt. Retain the lime wedge for use in the shaker.

Put the lime wedges in the bottom of a cocktail shaker and half fill with ice cubes. Pour in the tequila, Cointreau or Triple Sec and the lime juice. Shake well. Strain into the prepared cocktail glasses and serve.

Makes 6

bucks fizz

Try this with blood-orange juice for a nice change. You can squeeze your own in December and January, when the fruit is available, or buy cartons of juice the rest of the year.

375ml orange juice, chilled
1 bottle champagne or sparkling wine, chilled
grenadine (optional)

In each glass, mix the orange juice and champagne together, adding a dash of grenadine if liked. Serve immediately.

Variations
Try other juices: peach juice makes a 'bellini'; mango juice is also good.

A dash of crème de cassis with champagne or sparkling wine makes a kir royale.

Serves 6–8

sangrita

A touch of sweet and sour.

1 small onion, diced
300ml orange juice
1.2 litres tomato juice
juice of 4 limes
1 teaspoon Worcestershire sauce
1 teaspoon golden caster sugar
1 teaspoon Tabasco sauce
ice cubes
golden tequila

Place all the ingredients except the ice cubes and tequila in a liquidiser goblet, and whizz until smooth.

Place enough ice cubes into a large jug to fill it up to one third, then pour over a generous shot of tequila. Top up with the cocktail mixture, stir and serve.

Serves 6–8

fresh lemonade

Deliciously refreshing on a hot summer's day. To give it extra kick, add a shot of gin or vodka!

finely grated zest of 6 unwaxed lemons
juice of 12 lemons
175g golden caster sugar
ice cubes
soda water

Mix the lemon zest and juice with the sugar and stir until dissolved. If liked, add more sugar to taste. Cover and chill until required

When you are ready to serve the lemonade, place some ice cubes in large tumblers, pour some lemon syrup over and top up with soda water or iced water, to taste.

Serves 8–10

bloody mary

Begin making this cocktail the day before you want to drink it to allow the flavours to develop.

4 tablespoons Worcestershire sauce
1 tablespoon tomato ketchup
2 teaspoons Tabasco sauce
1 teaspoon celery salt
6 tablespoons lemon or lime juice
2 teaspoons grated horseradish
1 teaspoon finely chopped shallot
½ teaspoon ground black pepper
1.75 litres tomato juice
2 tablespoons dry sherry
300ml vodka
ice cubes
celery sticks, to garnish

Place all the ingredients except the vodka, ice cubes and celery in a liquidiser goblet and whizz until smooth. Transfer to a jug, cover and refrigerate overnight.

When ready to serve, strain the mixture through a fine sieve and stir in the vodka. Put some ice cubes into high-ball glasses and pour the bloody mary over. Garnish each glass with a celery stick.

Serves 8–10

6 tablespoons sultanas

a dash of brandy

200g golden caster sugar

pared zest of 1 orange

pared zest of 1 lemon

10 whole cloves

1 stick cinnamon

a grating of nutmeg

8 green cardamom pods, split

2 bottles red wine

Essential for winter barbecues. You can leave out the brandy-soaked sultanas if you prefer, but they make a surprise treat at the bottom of the glass!

Serves 6–8

Put the sultanas in a small bowl and just cover with brandy. Leave to soak while you prepare the spiced wine.

Put the sugar in a large saucepan with 600ml cold water and heat gently until the sugar is dissolved. Add the remaining ingredients except the sultanas and simmer for 20 minutes. Do not allow it to boil.

Put a few sultanas, if using, in each glass. Strain the spiced wine and pour into the glasses.

397g can condensed milk

150ml milk

seeds scraped from 1 vanilla pod

450g demerara sugar

100g unsalted butter, diced

This is not strictly a barbecue recipe, but an all-time favourite and just perfect for when you have put out the barbecue and are relaxing at the end of the meal with a cup of coffee.

Butter a shallow 20cm square tin. If preferred, line it with baking parchment to aid the removal of the fudge after it has set.

Put all the ingredients in a large non-stick saucepan over a low heat, and stir until the sugar has dissolved. Bring to the boil, stirring all the time, then simmer, stirring continuously for about 15 minutes until the mixture turns a rich caramel colour. Drop a small amount into a cup of iced water and it will turn into a soft ball between your fingers when it has reached the correct consistency.

When your fudge ball reaches this consistency, remove the pan from the heat and keep beating for 5–10 minutes until thickened. Pour into the prepared tin and leave to set. When firm, cut into squares.

conversion table

Weight (solids)	
7g	¼oz
10g	½oz
20g	¾oz
25g	1oz
40g	1½oz
50g	2oz
60g	2½oz
75g	3oz
100g	3½oz
110g	4oz (¼lb)
125g	4½oz
150g	5½oz
175g	6oz
200g	7oz
225g	8oz (½lb)
250g	9oz
275g	10oz
300g	10½oz
310g	11oz
325g	11½oz
350g	12oz (¾lb)
375g	13oz
400g	14oz
425g	15oz
450g	1lb
500g (½kg)	18oz
600g	1¼lb
700g	1½lb
750g	1lb 10oz
900g	2lb
1kg	2¼lb
1.1kg	2½lb
1.2kg	2lb 12oz
1.3kg	3lb
1.5kg	3lb 5oz
1.6kg	3½lb
1.8kg	4lb
2kg	4lb 8oz
2.25kg	5lb
2.5kg	5lb 8oz
3kg	6lb 8oz

Volume (liquids)	
5ml	1 teaspoon
10ml	1 dessertspoon
15ml	1 tablespoon or ½fl oz
30ml	1fl oz
40ml	1½fl oz
50ml	2fl oz
60ml	2½fl oz
75ml	3fl oz
100ml	3½fl oz
125ml	4fl oz
150ml	5fl oz (¼ pint)
160ml	5½fl oz
175ml	6fl oz
200ml	7fl oz
225ml	8fl oz
250ml (0.25 litre)	9fl oz
300ml	10fl oz (½ pint)
325ml	11fl oz
350ml	12fl oz
370ml	13fl oz
400ml	14fl oz
425ml	15fl oz (¾ pint)
450ml	16fl oz
500ml (0.5 litre)	18fl oz
550ml	19fl oz
600ml	20fl oz (1 pint)
700ml	1¼ pints
850ml	1½ pints
1 litre	1¾ pints
1.2 litres	2 pints
1.5 litres	2½ pints
1.8 litres	3 pints
2 litres	3½ pints

Length	
5mm	¼in
1cm	½in
2cm	¾in
2.5cm	1in
3cm	1¼in
4cm	1½in
5cm	2in
7.5cm	3in
10cm	4in
15cm	6in
18cm	7in
20cm	8in
24cm	10in
28cm	11in
30cm	12in

index

Acknowledgements

To my brilliant wife, Jacinta and our children, Toby and Billie, who suffered from my lack of quality time yet supported me throughout as I juggled everything else going on in my life.

To Louise Townsend, my energetic and ultra-efficient PA, Fiona Lindsay, Linda Shanks and Lesley Turnbull at Limelight Management and my great staff at my restaurants. To David Wilby, friend, business partner and operations director. To my friends who unwittingly tested some of the recipes over the long boozy barbecues that we held in the summer. To Jane Suthering, who had excellent input into these recipes. To David Matheson the photographer and Ben Masters who did the food styling for the stunning Aussie pictures. To Steve Lee who worked on them this side of the hemisphere. And finally to Muna Reyal, my editor and her fab team at Kyle Cathie.

I know it's great to use the barbecue all year and not just during the summer months – however to test these recipes has meant a lot of days in bitterly cold temperatures in the garden during the winter with all the help I could muster. My thanks have to go to all those friends and neighbours who have lit barbecues, helped to cook and taste and have even done all the washing up! (JS)

First published in Great Britain in 2006 by
Kyle Cathie Limited
122 Arlington Road, London NW1 7HP
general.enquiries@kyle-cathie.com
www.kylecathie.com

10 9 8 7 6 5 4 3 2 1

ISBN-13: 978 1 85626 663 5
ISBN-10: 1 85626 663 X

Antony Worrall Thompson and Jane Suthering are hereby identified as the authors of this work in accordance with Section 77 of the Copyright, Designs and Patents Act 1988.

Text © 2006 Antony Worrall Thompson, except for pp31 top, 64 top, 99 top, 105 bottom, 108 bottom, 121 top, 155 bottom © Jane Suthering
Photography © 2006 David Matheson, except for pp9, 14, 15, 20, 21, 42, 114–115, 132–133, 134, 136, 137, 141 © Steve Lee
Book design © 2006 Kyle Cathie Limited

Editorial Director Muna Reyal
Designer Carl Hodson
Photographer David Matheson
Food and prop stylist Ben Masters
Copyeditor Marion Moisy
Editorial Assistant Cecilia Desmond
Production Sha Huxtable and Alice Holloway

A Cataloguing In Publication record for this title is available from the British Library.

Colour reproduction by Sang Choy
Printed and bound in Slovenia by
MKT PRINT d.d.

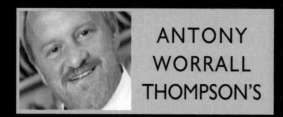

ANTONY WORRALL THOMPSON'S

Outdoor Living
BBQ & Patio Collection

Antony's BBQs are available in a variety of styles. From small and easily portable charcoal party models through to stainless steel, professional quality gas models. The barbecues are packed with innovative features and constructed using only the finest materials.

For details of available models and stockists:

web: **www.AWT-BBQ.com**

tel.: **0(+44)121 565 0110**

A collection of top quality barbecues, ranging from small charcoal to professional quality gas models.

OUTDOOR LIVING
RANGE BY

Antony Worrall Thompson